DYNAMIC
HEALTH

INSIGHT PUBLISHING
SEVIERVILLE, TENNESSEE

DYNAMIC
HEALTH

Disclaimer: This book is a compilation of ideas from numerous experts who have each contributed a chapter. As such, the views expressed in each chapter are of those who were interviewed and not necessarily of the interviewer or Insight Publishing.

Published by Insight Publishing Company
P.O. Box 4189
Sevierville, Tennessee 37864

10 9 8 7 6 5 4 3 2

Printed in The United States of America

ISBN: 1-60013-028-3

Table of Contents

A Message from the Publisher

Health is a hot topic today. Without good health, success in business and in personal life is difficult if not impossible to achieve. We need sound strategies on how to achieve good health and keep it. That's why we have gathered insights from several of today's top healthcare experts and presented them in this book. The interviews I conducted with these health professionals will provide you with information you can use to get healthy and stay that way.

I was interested but not surprised to find out that the latest research indicates a positive attitude directly affects health. I was intrigued to learn about why animals don't get ulcers and that this strategy is something we humans can learn and apply in our own life.

According to the twenty-ninth annual report on the health status of the nation prepared by the Secretary of the Department of Health and Human Services, as of 2005 life expectancy in the United States continues to show a long-term upward trend. This increased longevity is accompanied by an increase in chronic conditions such as arthritis, obesity, heart disease, hypertension, and many other disorders. It is up to us to take responsibility for our health and take pro-active steps to be informed about how our quality of life can be improved.

The conversations in this book will fascinate you and give you a new appreciation for how the human body is made and how it works. The health experts featured in *Dynamic Health* will give you trustworthy advice about how you can be healthy and stay healthy. All of us at Insight Publishing want to share with our readers the valuable tips these contributors have to offer so that you too can have dynamic health.

David E. Wright
President, International Speakers Network

Chapter 1

JACK SINGER

THE INTERVIEW

David Wright (Wright)

Dr. Jack Singer is a world-renowned psychologist, professional speaker, and consultant. The rich variety of his experiences ranges from using his expertise as a clinical hypnotherapist to helping patients with chronic illnesses eradicate their symptoms, to teaching athletes how to maximize peak performance skills, to even acting with Lucille Ball on her *Here's Lucy* television show!

Dr. Singer is a proud member of both the American Psychological Association and the National Speakers Association. Armed with a Ph.D. in Industrial/Organizational Psychology and a post doctorate in Clinical/Sports Psychology, Dr. Jack is a true expert who has spent the past twenty-five years consulting with and speaking for Fortune 1000 companies, events, and associations from Miami to Malaysia. Jack has also served on the faculties of six universities, including a wonderful stint as Assistant Professor of Psychology at the U.S. Air Force Academy.

A frequent guest on CNN©, MSNBC©, Fox Sports Net©, and countless radio talk shows, Jack's unique stress mastery techniques have also been featured in *USA-TODAY*©. Referred to as the "Patch Adams of Psychology," Jack is recognized among the world's leaders in promoting humor, fun, and laughter as the most powerful antidotes to stress and illness, both personally in the workplace. His undying passion is to teach all of his clients the real secrets for adding life to their years and years to their lives!

Jack, welcome to *Dynamic Health.*

Why did you want to be a contributor to this important book?

Dr. Jack Singer (Singer)

David, there have been wonderful research findings in the field of Clinical Psychology in the past ten years that have dramatically affected treatment of a variety of "medical" conditions previously considered solely in the realm of the physician. My passion is to show everyone the precise secrets for adding life to their years and years to their lives, both on and off their jobs!

Wright

What do you mean when you suggest that there are secrets for managing stress and protecting one's health?

Singer

It's remarkable that, based on their own research, even the American Medical Association acknowledges that about two out of every three patients who show up at a family practice or internal medicine physician's door actually do *not* have a physical ailment. They have real symptoms, but they don't have an organic disease causing those symptoms. Since physicians rarely have the time to really analyze their patients' socio-psychological history (which is where the causes of their stress and symptoms most often lie), doctors give their patients medication to deal with their symptoms. Consequently, most folks really do not understand the real causes of their symptoms, and they simply blunt their symptoms with medication.

So, when I say "the secrets for managing stress," I mean that, as a mental health provider, I understand where the sources of stress originate and that's what my role is—to help people understand this and to eliminate the precise cause of their stress. That process is sorely missing from the medical field.

Wright

So when there is really an organic cause, is that different from someone who just thinks they're ill?

Singer

It's not a question of just thinking you're ill—the symptoms are real. We know that a lot of symptoms, such as many pain symptoms for example, are real symptoms; but the symptoms can be brought on by emotional and stress-related reasons rather than just from an injury or underlying illness.

Frequently people will come to their doctor with pain in their lower abdomen, or with back problems, neck problems, etc. They are put through all kinds of tests such as X-rays, MRIs, etc. The tests may not provide an explanation, but the pain and the discomfort is real. That's when doctors usually simply treat their patients' symptoms with medication. The real problem is that no one is getting at the *source*, which includes the specific stressors in a person's life that are actually causing the symptoms.

Wright

In the last few years I've been reading a lot and hearing a lot about the immune system and how important it is. Would you tell us what the latest research shows about the immune system and emotions, etc.?

Singer

It's amazing, David. We actually now have a whole subgroup of psychologists called psychoneuroimmunologists. These are people who are trained to modify and enhance the immune system using psychological techniques. The reason this has come about is because there has been a ton of research in the last ten years or so showing that a person's immune system itself will either be enhanced because of good mental health or it will be beaten down because of a negative inner dialogue, for example. So the immune system itself is really sitting there just waiting to be made well if one can learn how to do that.

Wright

What is your view of the primary cause of stress for all of us?

Singer

We all have an "internal critic"—that little voice we have inside that is constantly speaking to us. About 97 percent of the things that little voice says to us are negative such as, "Don't take a chance on this," or, "What if this happens?" or, "People don't like me, so I'd better be careful," or, "My supervisor is probably angry," or, "I'm a failure as a parent." These are simple examples of messages we continually beat ourselves up with; just thinking such things can impact the immune system.

The way this works is when we think negative, self-defeating thoughts, it causes the alarm system inside our subconscious mind to turn on, as if there's a real threat to our survival, such as a person about to attack us. The subconscious mind doesn't really understand the difference between real threats to our safety and security and the ones we put in our heads because we're thinking negative, self-defeating thoughts.

For example, consider road rage: Someone is driving along the highway and he or she is cut off by another driver. This event infuriates the driver who is cut off. The subconscious mind doesn't know the difference between a rude, insensitive act and a life-threatening act, so it goes into full emergency mode. Multiply that event by the many frustrations we deal with on a daily basis and you can see the turmoil we are creating inside our bodies.

Wright

So, how does that emergency process ultimately affect our health?

Singer

Sadly, most people put themselves into this emergency mode many times a day because of the way they interpret events in their lives, such as having to wait in lines, or receiving the respect they think they're due, or their children's behavior being out of control. So, they're setting off their emergency system over and over again by telling themselves negative messages about everyday issues. We were not constructed to turn on our emergency system over and over; it was developed to turn on in real emergencies to help us survive. When the emergency ends, we relax and the system recovers. This constant switching on and off eventually wears down the immune system, which ultimately leads to the development of illness or the exacerbation of an already existing illness.

When you put your body into emergency mode (which your subconscious mind will do whenever you speak to yourself with negative, self-defeating thoughts), certain stress hormones are released that have a really deleterious affect on our health. For example, when the subconscious mind believes there is a true emergency, tightening of muscles is a rapid and natural response to deal with the "fight-or-flight" response necessitated by a real emergency. So, if people are tightening up muscles frequently during the day because their negative self-talk sets off their stress alarm, you can imagine how much muscle pain can be produced that is really not coming from a disease or injury at all.

Here's another example: When there is a true emergency, adrenalin pours into the bloodstream because you must be completely alert in order to deal with the situation. If the average person today is getting irritated frequently because of everyday stressors, then small amounts of adrenalin are being released into the bloodstream all during the day. The result of this is sleeping difficulty because of the presence of adrenalin; so insomnia is a natural result of allowing those stressors to get under your skin. This happens because you are not taking control of your internal dialogue.

I could go on and on about other "survival mechanisms" we put ourselves through on a daily basis. In each case, we engage those mechanisms because *we interpret everyday situations in a very negative way and our self-defeating internal dialogue—our internal critic, if you will—switches on the system.* Keep in mind that *events* that take place in our lives do not cause our stress; it is *our interpretation* of those events—our internal self-talk about those events—that ultimately determines whether we will be stressed or relaxed as each event progresses.

Consequently, the sad legacy for twenty-first century man is that the instinctive survival mechanism is engaged on a daily basis, ultimately causing many of the chronic health problems we develop and for which physicians can't find a purely medical cause.

Of course, animals don't go through self-dialogue, which is why they don't develop chronic diseases like humans do. Robert Sapolsky wrote a book titled, *Why Zebras Don't Get Ulcers.* The essence of this book is that animals only deal with *actual* emergencies. If a zebra is out on the plains grazing and it spots a lion in the brush, its emergency system switches on so that the zebra can protect itself. As soon as it outruns the lion or the lion goes somewhere else, the zebra goes back to grazing. It doesn't analyze what happens—it doesn't say, "What if this happens again?" It doesn't go through the mental gymnastics humans do that ultimately cause our bodies to continue to break down. That's why animals usually don't get ulcers, irritable bowel syndrome, etc. Simply put, we are the only creatures who have an "internal critic"—the source of our constantly switching on and off our emergency systems.

Using this logic, you can see how those of us who have a healthy internal dialogue on a regular basis have much better resiliency and can ward off illnesses or can recover much more quickly than those of us who are not in control of our internal dialogues.

Wright

You suggest that we are we programmed to think negatively early in our lives. How does that happen?

Singer

This is a remarkably tragic finding that a professor named Shad Helmstetter discovered in his research many years ago. Professor Helmstetter found that in this country the average youngster between the ages of six and eighteen is constantly hammered by well meaning but misinformed parents, teachers, and other authority figures. I am referring to negative comments, such as, "Don't take that risk," or, "You're not smart enough," or, "Don't go into that beauty contest because you're really not pretty enough," or, "You're not athletic enough so I wouldn't take a chance on this," or, "Let's be realistic, this isn't for you." Those are typical self-deflating comments by well-meaning people. Professor Helmstetter found that the average youngster in this country between the ages of six and eighteen is told those kinds of comments at least 148,000 times during that twelve-year span, versus hearing only 4,000 positives comments, such as, "Go for it; you can be anything you want to be," or, "Don't let anyone put you down," or, "Try it and you'll succeed." So with a ratio of 148,000 to 4,000 negative to positive comments, from folks we trust to know the truth, it's no wonder that so many of us don't have the confidence to pursue our dreams and we suffer from low self esteem.

As one of my mentors, Dr. Lee Pulos, says, "It's as if weeds are planted in the beautiful garden of our subconscious minds by these authorities figures. Then, tragically, we proceed to water and fertilize those weeds ourselves by repeating those same negative, self-defeating statements to ourselves over the years." This is how we are programmed to develop stress from early on and it is this negative, self-defeating internal dialogue that I refer to as the Internal Critic.

Wright

Would you tell our readers more about the Internal Critic?

Singer

We now know that most people speak about 55,000 words a day to themselves—300 words a minute. The unfortunate thing is, the vast majority of those words and phrases are negative—as I discussed earlier—such as, "What if this happens?" or, "I'm sure this person doesn't like me," or, "I'll never get all of my work done," or, "I'm feeling overwhelmed." These kinds of phrases are repeated over and over in our minds.

Other research shows us that it takes the body a full twenty-four hours to recover from *only five minutes* of negative self-talk. So, if it takes twenty-four hours to recover from five minutes of negative self-talk and if the vast majority of our internal dialogue is negative, then we're beating our bodies up continually with our "internal critics."

When I'm training people—whether during one of my speaking engagements or in my private practice—I always teach them how to understand the patterns of negative dialogue in which they engage and then I show them how to change those patterns. Changing your internal dialogue makes a miraculous difference—quickly.

Wright

You've already told us the importance of the immune system, but would you tell me, how does exposure to stress affect our immune systems?

Singer

As I mentioned earlier, stress hormones are constantly pouring into the blood stream. We know that stress hormones eventually break down the immune system. Think about this: from a survival standpoint, it makes sense that when the body believes it is being threatened, it diverts energy from long-term projects to deal with the emergency. For example, the immune system is not a necessary function during emergencies. Furthermore, the human body was not built for this emergency switch to be turned on and off many times each day; therefore, it is only a matter of time before a system breaks down under such repeated switching on and off.

A propensity toward irritable bowel syndrome (IBS) is one possible outcome of this repeated emergency system engagement. There is a body of research showing that folks who suffer from IBS are those who have constant, negative dialogues and avoid confrontations; therefore, they tend to allow themselves to be manipulated and others take advantage of them. Imagine, then, how often their emergency systems are turned on and off during the day.

As I mentioned earlier, one hormone that pours into our bloodstream when we're putting ourselves under stress is adrenalin. Adrenalin is necessary to make us alert and able to react to a real danger, but if you're constantly squirting adrenalin into your bloodstream because all during the day you're switching on your emergency system (via your internal critic), then you develop insomnia because the adrenalin keeps you awake and alert. Consequently, if you're constantly putting adrenalin into your bloodstream, you can't sleep and if you can't sleep, other parts of the body break down.

Wright

What does research show about the impact of optimistic thinking on our health?

Singer

This is a really fascinating field of work that has shown much promise in affecting our stress levels and health. Research in the last ten years or so, conducted primarily by Dr. David Seligman and his colleagues at the University of Pennsylvania, has shown that both the physical and emotional health of optimists are dramatically better than that of pessimists.

Let me explain further. We know that depression, grieving, and pessimism all worsen one's health. What begins as an unfortunate life event—loss of a spouse or job, an athletic defeat, a marital split—is accompanied by negative, internal self-talk, then feelings of helplessness. If one reacts to such events with pessimistic ideas and interpretations (i.e., assuming that the "blame" lies within himself or herself and it will never get better), then depression follows. Depression leads to the depletion of neurotransmitters and when that happens the immune system shuts down and disease is liable to follow.

Again, the key to this chain of events is the internal dialogue—the automatic thoughts we engage in when events take place. If our internal dialogue is pessimistic, then the ultimate result is a breakdown of the immune system.

On the other hand, when individuals look at negative events and their internal dialogue is optimistic, this leads to success and rapid recovery from those events. Interpreting these negative events as *temporary* setbacks, where the event is not indicative of their life (an optimistic explanatory style) leads to a healthy outcome, both physically and emotionally. These folks look at setbacks and defeats as challenges—temporary obstacles that can be overcome.

The good news here is that you can learn to be optimistic. Pessimistic thinking is not something you're stuck with for the rest of your life. You're not a prisoner of your past. You can actually learn to be optimistic and to view your environment and inevitable setbacks with an optimistic orientation. There are many books that teach people how to do that, including Seligman's book.

Wright

I'm really glad you're using the word "optimistic." The word "positive" works for a lot of people, but it doesn't work for me. People try to be positive rather than negative. It sounds good when you hear it for the first time, but optimistic suggests that when there is a negative situation, there is a possibility that you can work yourself through it.

Singer

That's a really good point. For example, let me just share a quick piece of research that Seligman and his associates did. They looked at professional basketball players throughout the entire National Basketball Association for a period of two years. They examined what players on all of the teams said after they lost a game. A pessimistic orientation is one where following a loss, you may explain it with such comments as, "We're really not that good this year. We have trouble in these kinds of games. We're rebuilding." Viewing your losses as permanent and chronic because "this is not your year and your team isn't that good" is a pessimistic orientation. The teams where the players make those kinds of comments almost always continue to lose.

On the other hand, an example of an optimistic explanatory style is when losing players make comments such as, "Well, this was a fluke; a couple of our players are injured, but they'll be coming back," or, "We have trouble in this arena, but that's the only place we seem to have trouble," or, "Don't worry, we'll bounce back." Statements like these mean that these players found a rational explanation for the loss and they didn't consider this to be their fault or a chronic problem.

Those teams almost always go on to victory. This is what's really important. If you have an optimistic orientation, you don't blame yourself for the problems you're having. Find other rational explanations for them, and you almost always will be healthier than the people who make statements like, "Yeah, I just need to face it; I'm this, I'm that. I'll never be good at this. I'll never do that." Those people beat themselves up pessimistically and their bodies ultimately break down, as well as their confidence, thus, their teams lose.

Wright

I was watching an NBA basketball game just this past week and this team lost. The announcer asked a player some questions and he replied, "Well, you know, we really played well tonight, but the other team just played better. They really played well, but we'll see what happens tomorrow night."

Singer

That's a typical example of an optimistic orientation. We find that those kinds of people are optimistic in all aspects of their lives. The critique on this is, *"You're just not accepting responsibility for your role when things don't go well."* That may very well be true. Maybe some optimistic people won't accept responsibility for their role when they do things wrong or when they fail to succeed, but it doesn't matter because the end result is these people are happier and healthier, and go most often succeed. In fact, when you look at cancer victims who take an optimistic orientation to their disease, they outlive the pessimistic ones who have the same disease. Hope and not accepting defeat seems to enable the body to rebound.

Wright

Will you talk to our readers a little bit about the power of humor on one's health?

Singer

Yes. This work all came about because many years ago a famous magazine publisher named Norman Cousins was diagnosed with a rare and serious collagen disease. He checked into the UCLA Medical Center. When the staff asked him what they could do to make his stay more comfortable, he said, "Well, I've always enjoyed The Three Stooges and the Marks Brothers; if you could get me some of their films, I'd really enjoy watching them." Of course, in Hollywood that was not a problem. So they brought in a projector and some films and Norman Cousins proceeded to laugh himself into health!

He became convinced that the uproarious laughter he experienced when he was watching the films was actually responsible for the reduction of his pain. He estimated that ten minutes of belly laughter brought him two hours of pain-free sleep. Miraculously, his disease went into complete remission and none of the medical people could explain it. It never came back again. He firmly believed that the reason was because of his laughing and he later funded a research center to study the effects of humor on pain and health. His experience is documented in his famous book, *The Anatomy of an Illness.*

Dr. William Fry, Jr., conducted much of the research and claims that mirthful laughter affects most of the major systems in the body. This "internal jogging" exercises everything from the cardiovascular system to the respiratory and muscular systems. Dr. Fry estimates that twenty seconds of hearty laughter gives the heart the same workout as three minutes of rowing. As you might guess, there is research that shows the close relationship between frequent laughing and positive immune functions.

When I first read this, I was a little skeptical. However, I saw it happen in my own family, where my father was on his deathbed in the intensive care unit of a hospital. His kidneys had failed him, he'd had a heart attack, and he was septic. My father had been the family comedian and he used humor in his sales job.

Since Dad was on a respirator, he couldn't really talk so he was using a clipboard to communicate. Suddenly, he started writing humorous things down on the clipboard—messages to the doctors, for example. One of the doctors asked, "I know this is a tough question, Mr. Singer, but you may be in your final days now. Are you interested in donating any organs?" Dad wrote back on the clipboard, "Well, I gave a piano away once; does that count?" The doctor and the nurses started laughing. Then Dad started feverishly writing funny, funny things on his clipboard and in four days, not only was he out of intensive care, but he was also out of the hospital! He'd laughed himself completely into health. It was like a miracle.

Research shows that there are many, many cases just like this.

Wright

Are there any other behaviors that research shows leads to improved health?

Singer

Yes. For example, we know that very positive benefits result when you assert yourself. Millions of people are afraid to assert themselves; and again, it's that "internal critic." They beat themselves up with statements like, "I don't want to embarrass this person," or, "I don't want to embarrass myself," or, "This person won't like me if I tell him how I feel." They use these as excuses to justify not asserting themselves, and therefore they get manipulated by people. This breaks down health because it adds stress. I always teach people how to assert themselves. A great book on this is, *Don't Say Yes When You Want to Say No* by Herbert Fensterheim, Ph.D. and Jean Baer. It starts with something very simple like sending your food back in a restaurant if it doesn't come prepared the way you ordered it (so many people are uncomfortable doing even that).

Another behavior that we understand enhances health is to forgive others—let go of resentment—forget about how someone has offended you and move on. This does not mean you need to remain close to these folks and expose yourself to more problems. Stay away from people who are constantly berating you and giving you messages that are not in your best interest. A lot of people who tend to be negative in the way they look at the world want you to join their "club." Unfortunately, we can be trapped in negative peoples' lives if they are relatives (i.e., parents and spouses). In those cases, just become a "Teflon person" and don't incorporate the negative messages those folks bombard you with.

Third, we now know that people who are spiritual—meaning having faith in anything—are usually quite healthy. So I tell people if they have neglected their spiritual health, (i.e., they haven't been to church in a while), think about getting back involved in it.

Next, thank a mentor and make a gratitude visit. What I mean by that is, think about your life and a person who had a huge impact on you. You have probably never really thanked that person because you didn't recognize it until years and years later. I tell people, if they can find these folks, call them on the phone, write them a letter, or if possible, pay them a personal visit. I did that myself a few weeks ago to a professor I hadn't seen in thirty years and it made both of us feel like a million dollars!

Practice random acts of kindness. People really feel better when they are kind to other people. Random acts of kindness can be anything from letting a harried mother get in front of you in line at the grocery store when you recognize she's having problems with her little ones, or bringing Sunday supper to an elderly neighbor when she doesn't expect it. If you're in a restaurant and notice a gentleman or a lady eating alone—perhaps they don't look particularly happy, maybe it's been a rough day or a rough week—call the waiter over and pay for their meal without letting them know you did it. Just do these kind acts randomly. It will make you feel wonderful.

Along with the last suggestion I would also recommend that you volunteer. Get involved in volunteer organizations because helping other people really makes you feel better about yourself.

Finally, the absolute number one ingredient for happiness in life, which translates itself to physical happiness as well as mental happiness, is maintaining strong relationships with family and friends. We know that people who have a strong relationship with family and/or friends are healthier. They recover from diseases much more quickly and they're much more mentally healthy, which means they're under much less stress. Even if you're not married, you can maintain strong relationships with extended family members and friends. Research shows that such relationships really help, so stay connected to someone.

Wright

Dr. Singer, I can't tell you how enlightening this has been for me, and I know it will be to our readers. I appreciate all the time you've spent here with me today.

Singer

It's my pleasure, David. My sole purpose is to give some pointers to your readers so that they will be able to change their lives in a magnificent way. As I mentioned earlier, these are called "secrets" because most folks don't realize how powerful these simple changes can be. Everyone is capable of implementing these ideas and the result will be a dramatic difference in their lives, both physically and mentally.

Wright

Today we've been talking with Dr. Jack Singer, a practicing Organization and Clinical and Sports Psychologist. He's an author, trainer, and consultant renowned for his innovative work in enhancing the immune system, overcoming stress, developing resiliency skills, and bringing fun to the workplace. I think we've all found out here today that he knows a lot about what he's talking about. Thank you so much, Dr. Singer, for being with me today on *Dynamic Health*.

Singer

It's my pleasure, anytime. And I encourage any of your readers to feel free to contact me with any questions. I can be reached at (949) 481-5660 or by e-mail, drjack@funspeaker.com

About The Author

DR. JACK SINGER is a practicing Organizational, Clinical, and Sports Psychologist, author, trainer, and consultant. His expertise includes a Doctorate in Industrial/Organizational Psychology and a Post-Doctorate in Clinical/Sports Psychology. He has been recognized with Diplomates from the American Academy of Behavioral Medicine, the Society of Police and Criminal Psychology, and from the National Institute of Sports. Jack has taught in the Psychology departments of seven universities, including four years as an Assistant Professor of Psychology at the U.S. Air Force Academy.

A proud member of both the American Psychological Association and the National Speakers Association, Jack is one of North America's top motivational speakers and he has spent twenty-five years speaking for and consulting with Fortune 1000 companies, athletes, professional associations, and human resources professionals from Miami to Malaysia. His research and self-help articles appear in business, medical, legal, human resources, and sports journals across the United States.

A sought-after media guest, Jack appears frequently on CNN, MSNBC, FOX-SPORTS, and on radio talk shows across the U.S. and Canada. Jack is renowned for his innovative work in enhancing the immune system, overcoming stress, developing resiliency skills, and bringing fun to the busy workplace. Referred to by many of his attendees as the "Patch Adams and Will Rogers of Psychology," Dr. Jack's amazingly successful interventions have even been featured in *USA-TODAY*.

Jack N. Singer, Ph.D.
President & CEO
Psychologically Speaking
28 Westcliff
Laguna Niguel, CA 92677
Phone: 800.497.9880
949.481.5660 (Voicemail)
Fax: 949.481.5027
E-mail: drjack@funspeaker.com
www.funspeaker.com

Chapter 2

DR. NORMAN ROSENTHAL

THE INTERVIEW

David E. Wright (Wright)

Today we are talking with Norman Rosenthal. He is best known as the psychiatrist and scientist who first described Seasonal Affective Disorder (SAD) or winter depression and pioneered the use of light in its treatment during his long and distinguished career as a National Institute of Mental Health researcher. For this work he was awarded the prestigious Anna Monica Award and International Prize for Research in Depression. He has conducted extensive research into disorders of mood, sleep, and biological rhythms, which resulted in over 200 scholarly publications.

Besides his scholarly writings, Dr. Rosenthal has also written several books for the general public, including Winter Blues, Seasonal Affective Disorder: What it is and How to Overcome it, and St. John's Wort, the Herbal Way to Feeling Good. Dr. Rosenthal's latest book is The Emotional Revolution: How the New Science of Feelings Can Transform Your Life.

Dr. Rosenthal's skill at communicating complex scientific material in a way that is both readily understandable and engaging has made him a popular television and radio guest. He has appeared on many national shows including *Good Morning America, CBS Sunday, CBS*

Morning News, CNN, Fresh Air, All Things Considered, ESPN, and *The Today Show,* just to name a few.

Dr. Rosenthal is the medical director of Capital Clinical Research Associates and maintains an active private practice in suburban Maryland. He has been listed among the best doctors in America and in the *Guide to America's Top Psychiatrists.*

Dr. Norman Rosenthal, welcome to *Dynamic Health.*

Dr. Norman Rosenthal (Rosenthal)
It's good to be with you again.

Wright
Dr. Rosenthal, Seasonal Affective Disorder (SAD) is a fascinating subject. How long have you been engaged in the study of SAD and light therapy?

Rosenthal
A little over twenty years ago, the whole concept of Seasonal Affective Disorder came together for me. I had come from South Africa to the United States, and here—much further away from the equator—I felt the seasonal changes in my own mind and in my own body. Then when I saw other people who experienced similar changes, the pieces of the jigsaw puzzle came together, with the help of my colleagues. We then officially described "Seasonal Affective Disorder"—a condition of regular winter depressions. That was a good twenty years ago.

Wright
You know, most of my life I have lived where there were four distinct seasons, and I've always felt differently in each one. I thought it was caused by the memory of events such as swimming in the summer, hiking in the fall, or sledding in the winter. Why do I really feel differently as the seasons change?

Rosenthal
Well, seasons are so rich and so complex; it's hard to pinpoint exactly one thing. I think they provide us with tremendous variety. I have heard about people who have lived in very temperate areas where the seasons change and then move to the tropics or closer to the equator and then say they really miss the seasons—they miss the diversity and the richness. So I think we cannot exclude memories—

the things we do at different seasons, the changing colors, the changing feelings and smells, and the sights of the different seasons.

We also need to remember that seasons have a powerful effect on our biology just like they do on many of the animals we see around us—the squirrels, the bears—the very seasonal animals that breed at different times of the year. Although we have thought we've escaped our environment, we humans remain very locked and have actual changes in our mood, in our bodies, in our biology, and in our brain chemistry in the different seasons.

Wright

You have said that the pain of depression, anxiety, and other emotional disturbances is as real as physical pain. It deserves to be understood, studied, treated, healed, and reimbursed by insurance just like the pain of any other illness. I know your pioneering work in the field of SAD and life therapy has helped in the identification and treatment of seasonal depression in people; but do the insurance companies recognize these advances and do they cover them?

Rosenthal

This is a sad fact of American life—firstly, there are so very many people who don't have medical insurance at all; but even among those who do, there is a double standard whereby patients with so-called recognized physical illnesses get properly reimbursed or reimbursed at a higher rate than patients with mental illnesses who are reimbursed at a very low rate. Members of Congress have tried to turn it around, but so far their efforts have been unsuccessful. As a psychiatrist who sees the pain that conditions like depression or schizophrenia cause human beings it seems just plain wrong to me that these patients are not reimbursed at comparable rates to other kinds of illnesses.

Wright

Someone told me in an interview a few months ago that the pharmaceutical industry financed almost everything in the medical community. That shouldn't make any difference, should it? I mean, the pharmaceutical companies would come into play with medicine for anxiety and that sort of thing just as much as for the pain of ulcers, wouldn't they?

Rosenthal

Indeed, the pharmaceutical companies are a huge power in developing new forms of treatment, and I think we are quite indebted to them for coming up with many novel medications. Of course, Prozac and Zoloft (just to name two) have been huge bestsellers along with many others as well (I won't list them all). But these, of course, have come out of research that is funded by the pharmaceutical companies, so I think that they have a lot to offer. To some degree the pharmaceutical companies all stay powerful, however, and that should be balanced against government funding of research, which is also very important.

Wright

One of your clients has written, and I would like to quote here, "For years my mood energy dropped with the leaves, and I felt ashamed and saddened by my inability to control my winter depression. Dr. Rosenthal's book, *Winter Blues*, gave me the tools to effectively treat SAD. Now my winters are productive and happy." What tools do you give your readers in your book, *Winter Blues?*

Rosenthal

The first tool I try to give my readers is just self-awareness—to understand how their moods are changing with the changing seasons. I think insight and knowledge is power when it comes to the brain as in other aspects of life. Once they know what they are suffering from in the case of winter depression, they can plan, they can prepare, and they can use some of the techniques that have been found helpful like increasing their environmental light, exercise, stress management, and dietary control. In some people medications may also be extremely helpful.

Wright

You've been internationally recognized for your work in depression research and you are listed as one of the best doctors in America and in the *Guide to America's Top Psychiatrists.* How prevalent is depression in the United States? How does it negatively affect our lives?

Rosenthal

The National Institute of Mental Health has posted on their web site that approximately 18.8 million American adults, or about 9.5 percent of the U.S. population age eighteen and older in a given year, have a depressive disorder (June 2005 figures). This is really a huge number.

Wright

Eighteen *million*?

Rosenthal

Yes, it's a huge number and there's also evidence that depression is occurring more often in younger people, which of course takes a huge toll on the country in so many ways. They've also estimated the cost of depression to the society to be more than forty-three billion dollars per year both in terms of the cost of treatment and in terms of lost productivity, absenteeism, or what they've called "presenteeism." Presenteeism is a term that means a person is there at work but is really unable to be properly engaged in productive efforts.

Wright

Is it caused by stress?

Rosenthal

Stress can certainly bring it on. Loss can bring it on. There's also evidence of a genetic basis to depression. I also think a lack of community and a lack of good things in a person's life can precipitate depression. Many factors can bring on depression. In the case of winter depression, the lack of light can do it; so there are many ways whereby somebody can become depressed.

Wright

Why do you think that it is beginning to affect people at a younger age?

Rosenthal

This is really not known. One thing that's been raised as a possibility is drug use. Certainly drugs can induce depression. People have suggested that perhaps young people are less connected with their families and their communities, which are protective influences perhaps in the development of depression. But these are some factors that come into play.

Wright

I cannot remember a time when I was a young boy that I did not eat meals with my family, and now I have a teenager and most of the time we do not eat together.

Rosenthal

Well, I think that really does say something, doesn't it?

Wright

It gives me something to think about, I'll tell you. Let's talk about light therapy. First of all, what is light therapy? How does light affect us?

Rosenthal

Well, of course, light is critical for enabling us to see. What's really quite new over the last couple of decades is the idea that light has important biological effects on us over and above enabling us to see. One of these effects seems to be to maintain our mood and energy level and that's why, when light levels decline in the fall and in the winter months, some people who are sensitive to this lose energy and have a decline in their mood.

Light therapy is simply an attempt to replace the missing light. This is done by means of special light fixtures, which are boxes with fluorescent tubes filtered by a plastic diffusing screen. These lights have been shown in research studies to be highly effective in reversing the symptoms of winter depression.

Wright

Are these the same fluorescent bulbs that we can go down to our friendly Wal-Mart store and buy, or is it special light?

Rosenthal

The tubes themselves can be regular off-the-shelf tubes. The trick, however, is to have a lot of light packed into one place, because it seems that the *amount* of light is very important. Also the timing of light can be very important, and light treatment in the morning seems to be the most effective type of treatment for most people.

Wright

I found a few places on the Internet that sell "light boxes" or "dawn simulators." I didn't know what they were. Are these the tools you recommend, and do they work for everyone suffering from SAD?

Rosenthal

Yes, indeed. There are some companies that manufacture light boxes. I have listed them on my Web site. In case your listeners or readers would like to visit the site, it is www.normanrosenthal.com. There is a link on my site to light box companies that have been around for many years, whose products follow certain guidelines, and who stand behind their work. For people with SAD these lights can be extremely helpful, but you know, nothing works for *everybody*. That's why it's always good to have some tricks up your sleeve.

For some people the lights may be somewhat helpful, but might not do the entire job. Those people may require medications as well as light therapy. For other people the lights may be a nuisance to have to use. For them it's also a comfort to know that other treatments are available.

Wright

Would it also help to be out of doors more often early in the morning when there is light rather than staying in the house?

Rosenthal

Definitely. I recommend that people go for morning walks and I follow my own advice. I feel that it's a very good thing to combine aerobic exercise with exposure to light. Walking around the neighborhood—if it is a safe neighborhood—is another way of linking oneself to the community and having that combination of social contact with light and exercise—combining all these healthy and pleasurable influences together.

Wright

Many people around the world became acquainted with you because of your study of the herb St. John's Wort and its effect on emotional health. For those of us who don't know much about this herbal remedy, will you tell us a little bit about your findings?

Rosenthal

Yes. It's intriguing to think that the extract of a plant can actually improve our mood, but in fact, St. John's Wort is really the oldest documented antidepressant around. There is an Italian chemist named Angelo Sala who, 350 years ago, carefully documented how he would give the extract of St. John's Wort to melancholic people—people who suffered from depression—and how it seemed to be specifically helpful to depressed people. Then in Germany in the early part of the twentieth century, interest about St. John's Wort resurged and a lot of research was done. By now there are many, many studies that show the effect of St. John's Wort—that it is an active antidepressant and should be considered as one of many options for people suffering from depression.

Wright

When it comes to herbal remedies and treatments, there seems to be two camps. Some people are completely open-minded about the positive effect of certain actual treatments and give credible personal testimony. Others seem to be completely close-minded. Is there a correlation in the scientific community to a person's predisposition about the effectiveness of herbal medicine and actual clinical effectiveness?

Rosenthal

Remember that the idea of medications coming from herbs is nothing new. Digitalis comes from foxglove, and an anticancer drug came from the plant called little periwinkle. So the idea that plants are sources of potent medications is not a new thing.

I guess one factor at work here is that there was an Act passed by which herbs and dietary supplements are not regulated like medications. What this really means is that it's hard really to know what you are getting when you purchase herbal extracts because they are not standardized—they aren't required to conform to a set of pre-set standards like the recognized medications/pharmaceuticals are. They don't always have as much of the herb extract in them, and they are not easily patentable. There isn't the commercial incentive to study them as rigorously. Those are the problems in terms of knowing exactly what's what with herbs; but by the same token they probably have tremendous value in some instances.

As I said, St. John's Wort is healthful with mood. Kava kava is an herb that's helpful for anxiety although recently there have been some reports of liver damage with that herb, which justifiably scares people away from it. But here again, if it was a pharmaceutical product, the company would swoop in and figure out how to prevent any damage and produce a safe product. Now, since it is not a regulated product, there's a halo of discomfort that surrounds it because of reports of liver damage. Valerian root is a good aid for sleep. So many herbs can affect the mind in positive ways; it's just that you're not quite sure what you are getting with the preparations.

Wright

I take saw palmetto.

Rosenthal

It's an herb helpful for prostate health.

Wright

Yes. I take that religiously at least twice a day. I read an article just a few days ago that another thing that helps enlarged prostate is pumpkin seeds. The writer advised going to the health store to find them. I went to the health store and, of course, they didn't have them. I don't know about any empirical evidence, but the testimony of people who were using it (anecdotal evidence) was fantastic. The real problem with an enlarged prostate is you have to get up to go to the bathroom several times a night. Saw palmetto helped considerably and if anything else would help, I would certainly be open to taking it.

Rosenthal

There is certainly data in relation to saw palmetto. I don't know about the pumpkin seeds.

Wright

In the last decade, I've notice more and more breakthroughs in medical research that contradicts long-standing beliefs about health and medicine. I'm certain that you've been a part of some of this research. How can I, an average person with limited understanding of these things, know what is real and what is "snake oil"?

Rosenthal

I still believe that science is a critical method for separating the real from the illusory. I think that we should go with things that are scientifically backed. That having been said, sometimes science just isn't there yet and we still may need to go with our own experience or the experience of those we respect in deciding how best to lead our lives.

Wright

Dr. Rosenthal, do you have an overriding personal philosophy of health that you could share with our readers?

Rosenthal

Yes. I believe that we need to keep our intellectual mind, our emotional mind, and our body in line. These are the three domains we need to take care of. If we take care of all those we have the best chance, not only of leading long lives, but of leading good and healthy ones as well.

Wright

Before we close, would you tell us what is on the horizon for Dr. Norman Rosenthal?

Rosenthal

Well, I would follow up on what I think leads to a healthy life by outlining how I am personally going to try to pursue that. In terms of physical health, I exercise regularly and I have started Yoga, which is a wonderful form of exercise, so different from the Western way of thinking. Yoga emphasizes relaxation and stretching and moment-to-moment consciousness of being, which I think are each tremendously valuable. So I am careful with exercise, with Yoga, with diets, and of course with regular checkups with my own physician—all the ordinary things that Western medicine can give us now. For example, we've now learned that lowering cholesterol is very valuable and that the drugs that do it—the Statins—can have all sorts of unexpected payoffs. So that's the physical peace.

Regarding emotional peace, I feel it's very important to identify the meaningful people in one's life, keep in touch with them, and have a constructive connection. If there are people who are important to you whom you really care about, but there's been a falling out, I think if you should "mend your fences;" that's a good thing. I think it's so unhealthy to carry anger and negative feelings about with you if you don't have to. To divest yourself of that is really good and to dwell in a positive zone. These are things that I personally try and follow. I think they are not any good for our bodies but they're good for our souls.

Personally love an adventure, and writing my books has been a huge adventure for me. But now I've embarked upon an adventure that is both new and old. I am back to doing research. Basically I am testing new medications for various psychiatric illnesses and I am also eager to continue to study the effects of our physical environment on our brains and our bodies; it's an intriguing thing to me. I had left research for three or four years and now that I am back in it again, I feel like a Labrador that's been let loose in the water! It's so much fun, and I am eager to both discover and contribute at the same time. These are some of the things that I hope to have in store for me.

Wright

Well, that's good news for those of us who will be recipients of that work, I can assure you. I certainly appreciate all the time that you have taken with me today, Dr. Rosenthal. It's always a pleasure to talk with you. Before the interview started I told my wife I had an interview to do and she asked me whom I'll be speaking with. When I said, "Dr. Norman Rosenthal," she said, "Uh oh! He is one of your favorites. You respect him as much as anybody." And she's right about that.

Rosenthal

Well, I think you and I have a mutual admiration society going because I remember after our last conversation feeling quite elated for hours afterwards because you are so enlivening and so positive. One ends up feeling so good having spoken with you. Are you sure you weren't a therapist in a previous incarnation?

Wright

That could be!

Rosenthal

Any time, any time. I look forward to continuing our conversations over the years.

Wright

Thank you so much for being with us Dr. Rosenthal.

Today we've been talking with Dr. Norman Rosenthal, who is best known, of course, as a psychiatrist, but also as the scientist who first described SAD—Seasonal Affective Disorder—or winter depression; and as we have learned today, quite knowledgeable on that and other topics as well. Thank you so much, Dr. Rosenthal.

Rosenthal
Have a good day.

About The Author

DR. NORMAN ROSENTHAL is best known as the psychiatrist and scientist who first described seasonal affective disorder (SAD) or winter depression, and pioneered the use of light in its treatment during his long and distinguished career as a National Institute of Mental Health researcher. For this work he was awarded the prestigious Anna Monika Award, an international prize for research in depression. He has conducted extensive research into disorders of mood, sleep and biological rhythms, which resulted in over 200 scholarly publications.

Besides his scholarly writings, Dr. Rosenthal has also written several books for the general public, including *Winter Blues: Seasonal Affective Disorder: What it is and how to overcome it* (Guilford, 1998); *How to Beat Jet Lag: A Practical Guide for Air Travelers* (Holt, 1993; co-author); and *St. John's Wort: The Herbal Way to Feeling Good* (HarperCollins, 1998). His latest book is *The Emotional Revolution: How the New Science of Feelings can Transform Your Life* (Kensington, 2002).

Dr. Rosenthal's skill at communicating complex scientific material in a way that is both readily understandable and engaging has made him a popular television and radio guest. He has appeared on many national shows including *Good Morning America, CBS Sunday, CBS Morning News,* CNN, *Fresh Air, All Things Considered,* ESPN and *The Today Show.*

Dr. Rosenthal is the medical director of *Capital Clinical Research Associates* (CCRA) and maintains an active private practice in Suburban Maryland. He has been listed among *The Best Doctors in America* and in the *Guide to America's Top Psychiatrists.*

Dr. Norman Rosenthal
E-mail: nermd@normanrosenthal.com

Chapter 3

Todd E. Curzie, DC, LCP, DPhCS

THE INTERVIEW

David Wright (Wright)
Today we're talking with Todd E. Curzie, DC, LCP, DPhCS. A graduate of Palmer College of Chiropractic (the founding college of Chiropractic in Davenport, Iowa), he is honored to have been in the first class to graduate during the centennial year of Chiropractic. He completed his undergraduate studies at La Salle University in Philadelphia, Pennsylvania, where he received a Bachelor of Arts degree in Biology with a minor in Psychology.

Dr. Curzie is also an inaugural member of the Palmer Legion of Chiropractic Philosophers, a prestigious degree obtained to continue to uphold the founding principles of Chiropractic.

Todd, welcome to *Dynamic Health*.

Todd Curzie (Curzie)
Thank you. It is always a great pleasure to talk about chiropractic.

Wright
What is the major difference between chiropractic care and medical care?

Curzie

When we talk about chiropractic we must understand the major premise behind it. Chiropractic is a philosophy, science, and art of things natural. Defined by R. W. Stephenson, DC, PhC, in his 1927 textbook on Chiropractic, he said it was a system of adjusting the segments of the spinal column by hand only for the correction of the cause of dis-ease. What we chiropractors call "dis-ease" is a lack of ease, a lack of normal flow of a thing called the mental impulse. It is in a completely different realm than that of the medical world. It must be understood that the mental impulse is an abstract concept. We are a vitalistic component of health care and the medical world is the mechanistic version of health care. Vitalism versus mechanism needs to be studied in great length to truly understand our philosophy.

The main purpose of chiropractic is to correct subluxation, which is the misalignment of bones that puts pressure on nerves resulting in dis-ease. The main purpose of the medical profession is to chemically alter the body.

Wright

What is the major source of healing? If drugs do not heal, then what does?

Curzie

It comes back to the thing we call "innate intelligence." We know the body has an inborn potential to heal and because we're given this intelligence from the Creator, we have the ability to heal and the ability to adapt. We have universal intelligence throughout the world—everything has an intelligence in it. We, as living beings, have innate intelligence—an intelligence within our bodies that allows the body to heal if there is no interference in the body. As doctors of chiropractic we work to remove the interference and make sure the body has the ability to heal and work at its optimum potential.

Wright

You used a term I'd never heard before. Will you explain more about innate intelligence?

Curzie

Innate intelligence is that inborn intelligence that allows our body to adapt to the environment all the time. Innate intelligence is that perfect intelligence given to us by what we call the "universal intelligence." Universal intelligence is in all matter and continually gives to matter all its properties and actions, thus maintaining it in existence. Therefore everything has universal intelligence. We, as living beings, have that inborn intelligence—that innate intelligence which is life. Our job as chiropractors is to release that innate intelligence and allow our bodies to heal. Innate cannot function properly if there is interference caused by a subluxation. Again, the mental impulse— that abstract entity of that impulse—operating over the nervous system going to every single cell in the body—that "electromagnetic field," if you will, is responsible for health. Innate is health. That is a primary element in chiropractic.

Wright
What is your philosophy on pain management?

Curzie
Unfortunately, pain management is where everyone in health care is going. Everybody wants to deal with pain and the problems it causes. It's not necessarily about the pain. As chiropractors we see that pain is definitely a great motivator to get people to notice they have a problem. Many people come in to our office because of the various kinds of pain they have—they want to find relief. Within the various fields of medicine there are drugs that can relieve pain. However, if we take away the body's ability to recognize pain, we are taking away the body's ability to heal. The body needs pain as a sign that something is wrong

What we as chiropractors do is work with the body's nervous system. We make sure our patients understand that pain is a sign that healing needs to take place and if we can release the body's ability to heal, the pain will no longer be there and then they can function as the body was intended to function.

Within the last 111 years of chiropractic, people who go to chiropractors discover that their pain goes away very quickly. Relief of pain under chiropractic care is not a long process. It's the reconstructive and the rehabilitative phases of the nervous system, not just the musculoskeletal system, that takes time. We want to make sure the body is functioning properly, not just eliminate pain. If you fool the body's intelligence by altering it's chemical state, there will be side effects.

Wright

Is there any one "right" answer for healthy living?

Curzie

Yes, chiropractors say that innate intelligence *is* health. To live a healthy life you must have that innate intelligence flowing—you must have it working properly. It will always work 100 percent properly without interference. There may be no one way to be perfect unless you do all things right—nutrition, positive mental attitude, exercise—there are many things you have to do right at the same time. It is in the chiropractic philosophy where we recognize that the innate is the healer and that Innate is health. If we are striving for dynamic health, we must have that dynamic innate intelligence keeping us active at all times and keeping us adapting. Nature needs no help, just no interference.

Wright

The title of this book is *Dynamic Health*. In your opinion, what is the secret to dynamic health?

Curzie

Life and motion are inseparable. In order to have true, dynamic health there must be movement to be alive. We have never seen a dead thing move so we know that there must be that intelligence—that life and movement—coming through the matter we know as our body.

As chiropractors we like to not only keep the spinal column moving but we like to keep the body adapting and being in a dynamic state. When we stop being dynamic we are at an equilibrium and equilibrium is death—the loss of adaptability. Therefore, death is the inability to adapt.

Wright

Will you give our readers some idea of what you think the key to being a catalyst of health is?

Curzie

The key to being a good chiropractor is knowing you are not the healer—the body is the healer—and we are just a catalyst to health. This is a huge difference between the chiropractic and medical fields. We put a force into the body; the body takes that force and redirects it. By the "body" I mean innate intelligence. Innate intelligence is going to take over and do the healing, whereas I am just a force into the body—another universal force coming into the body. The body has to take that force and adapt it. In order to be a good catalyst you have to recognize you are not doing the healing. You have to be in tune with the patient's body, you have to be there in present time with the patient, but you cannot think that as their doctor you are going to take all their troubles away. There are constructive and destructive forces constantly working on the body from the environment. The body reacts to these plusses and minuses and the sum or outcome happens to be that person's point of health. A good chiropractor is another huge plus in favor of the patient's health.

Wright

I remember, just a few years back, I was in some tremendous pain for over a long period of time. I considered going to a chiropractor. Before that I thought they were one step above witch doctors. I decided to try it and in two or three visits, to my surprise, my pain was gone. Not only was my pain gone, but my chiropractor told me how to keep it away and now I do that almost every day. I would say that was a miracle; you might not call that a miracle—

Curzie

I call every "little" result like that a miracle. It happens every day.

Wright

Will you tell us some of the dynamic health miracles you have experienced in your practice?

Curzie

I really love the children I take care of in my practice because they respond so well and so completely. We had a little girl here the other day; I happened to be up in the front of the office and I asked her how her daughter was. She said, "I don't know how to repay you." The medical doctors told her she had almost complete hearing loss and she was being fitted for hearing aids. She was adjusted just a couple of times. When they went back to do the computerized testing they said her daughter had no difficulty in hearing and she does not need hearing aids.

Not only does it give me chills to be a part of that story, but I laughed because Daniel David (D. D.) Palmer gave the first chiropractic adjustment in September 18, 1895, to Harvey Lillard who had complained of hearing problems for seventeen years. After three adjustments, Lillard's hearing was restored. D.D. always said that his adjustment was never repeated, but I think I came close to a repeat after adjusting that little girl.

That's but one of the "little" miracles we see as chiropractors, however, they are huge to that particular patient. Some people are carried into the office and they walk out. Every chiropractor has experienced these miracles—they are just so common.

The fewer drugs and toxins the body has in its system, the better the body responds. "Miracles" happen more often with less destructive forces working against us.

Wright
Will you tell our readers a little bit about the history of chiropractic?

Curzie
Chiropractic has been around for over a 110 years. It started with D. D. Palmer who was working on a new system of healthcare. He actually started his work in 1885 but didn't get to utilize it for a decade. As I mentioned earlier, the first chiropractic adjustment was performed on Harvey Lillard in Davenport, Iowa, on Second and Brady Streets in the Ryan Building on September 18, 1895. Harvey was working as a janitor and owned a janitorial service there. One day while he was working in a stooped position he heard something pop in his neck. He complained of deafness for seventeen years after that.

Palmer rationalized that there was pressure on the nerve responsible for hearing thereby causing Lillard's hearing loss. He thought if he could remove that pressure—remove that interference—the man would become well. Harvey said he was so deaf he couldn't hear the rattle of wagon wheels on the cobblestone streets below. After three consecutive adjustments to Harvey's spine, he was able to hear again. Chiropractic was never about low back pain, although it is now recognized to be the premier choice for low back pain sufferers and one of the major reasons most people seek chiropractic care. If they only knew how many benefits there really are from receiving chiropractic care!

B. J. Palmer DC, PhC, took chiropractic to new heights. He took his father's work and brought it to the masses. He wrote many books on chiropractic and continues to be recognized as ahead of his time with his research and theories.

Chiropractic has been through a lot of ridicule and abuse. However, it continues to thrive. It is often referred to as alternative medicine but people visit their chiropractor more than any other provider. Chiropractors soon learn that sticking to pure chiropractic principles will bring the most results to their patients. It is the history of chiropractic and its thirty-three principles that drive me to be one of the great chiropractic philosophers who reinforce these principles, lifting the discipline to a higher standard.

Wright

What is the relationship of nutrition to good health?

Curzie

Good nutrition is a huge part of healthy living. We live in a world with bioengineered foods and many toxins in our system. If we're going to maintain healthy living we need to decrease the amount of destructive components in our life and make sure we are living with an intake of nutritious foods, supported by a continual outflow of positive thoughts. Without proper nutrition the body has to fight all those toxins—it has to fight all the unhealthy things coming in. Good nutrition would benefit the body's innate intelligence so it can work properly. There are three things that cause a subluxation: thoughts, traumas, and toxins. Poor nutrition is a toxin we can prevent on a daily basis.

Wright

I'm interested in what you said a few moments ago about movement. What is the relationship of dynamic health to movement?

Curzie

As I mentioned, life and motion are inseparable. When we stop moving and stop adapting we reach a stage called death—the failure to adapt. We have to continuously move and adapt. We live in a pretty stagnant society with computers and television. Many people just sit for hours on end. We need to have inner segmental movement throughout the spinal column, especially the upper cervical region—the top of the neck. The nervous system starts in the brain. From there it travels along the spinal cord and innervates every single cell in the body. Every single cell in the body is controlled by nerves. We have to have that continuous flow of intelligence without interference. We can't have interference of the mental impulse. Restriction of movement will restrict health.

Wright

I know this is a loaded question that you might not want to even get involved with, but what is your opinion about the future of health care?

Curzie

I think Thomas Edison said it very well. He said, "The doctor of the future will give no medicine, but will educate his patients in the care of the human frame, in diet, and in the cause and prevention of disease."

We, as a society, are moving more toward trying to figure out what is going to keep us healthy, just as your chiropractor gave you steps to keep you pain free. We need to look at ourselves—not receiving healing from outside sources, but healing from within. We're really going toward that now.

Many say that chiropractic is a complementary and alternative medicine. It is really not complementary to anything. Chiropractic is a primary health care system. In order to see that, we have to shift our paradigm and understand that our body has intelligence, we don't need drugs to heal, we don't need outside sources to heal.

Certainly we have to do things to prevent certain physical problems from getting out of control. A chiropractor does not expect that someone who is in the end stages of cancer will become cancer free with adjustments. We recognize that momentum of certain conditions may be too great to overcome. The body has limits. But I think future doctors will emphasize prevention and a healthier lifestyle in general. Hopefully we'll see the end of the unhealthy foods served in the fast food restaurants that are killing us by the mouthful, one bite at a time.

Wright

Is there a major internal conflict that many chiropractors face in what we call the "real world of business"?

Curzie

Looking at the insurance industry, patients wonder if it will pay for chiropractic care. We're also faced with pain, but again, healing is not about just stopping pain. But pain, the great motivator, will encourage people to come to a chiropractor to get relief. At the same time we're going to look at the bigger picture of health. I think a lot of chiropractors are looking at the money, whereas if we all stayed with the major goal of chiropractic—to remove subluxation—we wouldn't be going off in five hundred different directions and there wouldn't be disillusionment about what real chiropractic is.

One of the reasons why I extended my education to become one of the first thirty-seven diplomats in chiropractic philosophy is to make sure that we try to maintain our profession as a separate and distinct healthcare discipline. In order to do that I think we need to come together at some level and examine what it is we really do.

Not focusing on the major goal of chiropractic—removing subluxation—and getting into other things for other reasons such as money is the foremost problem in the profession today.

Wright

What is a Chiropractic Philosopher and why would you spend so much time getting a degree in this specialty?

Curzie

A Chiropractic Philosopher loves chiropractic! The 1960s was the last time the degree of Philosopher of Chiropractic (PhC) was offered. Now, a chiropractor can conduct over a year's study to become inducted into the Legion of Chiropractic Philosophers. We recently just finished a four-year study in the Philosophical Chiropractic Standards. The DPhCS is the new PhC.

What we'd like to promote is the future of the profession of chiropractic, making sure we guard it as a separate and distinct profession and make sure we continue to keep chiropractic pure and based on its fundamental principles. We want to keep the removal and prevention of subluxation as the crux of the discipline.

Wright

Why would our readers go to a doctor of chiropractic?

Curzie

The reason to go to a chiropractor is to function at your optimum potential. It is not just to relieve pain. Chiropractic can enable the body to be an absolute fighting machine that can take the forces of the environment and adapt to it instead taking drugs and making the environment adapt to the body. It is a way to obtain dynamic health.

Chiropractors want to make sure your body is resistant to opportunistic organisms that can make you sick when your body is subluxated—when your body is not functioning normally. In disease and crisis care when you're sick, the medical community fights those things and tries to get rid of them from outside in. Chiropractic can work from the inside out to get you to function at your best. We all have the ability to be healthy and we all have health inside each of us. Again, health is innate and innate is health.

We need to be able to recognize that we have the ability to be healthy. By going to a chiropractor you are one step closer to a more dynamic life.

Wright

Why do doctors of chiropractic wish to remain a separate and distinct entity?

Curzie

That's a good question. Often we're asked why we wouldn't want to be recognized by the American Medical Association (AMA) and why we wouldn't want to be a part of their group. If a patient comes to us with a problem beyond the scope of chiropractic, we refer them to a medical doctor—we make sure we stay on our side of the road. Again, as chiropractic philosophers, we are trying to keep our chiropractic brothers and sisters on our side of the road. We want to make sure that we are doing our thing while the medics do their thing. We do not want to lose our identity. If we lose our philosophy we lose everything.

There is an art and skill to chiropractic. It is not just removing pressure on a nerve. Everything we do is backed by science. There is a large amount of research on chiropractic and its accomplishments. It takes a long time to learn—learning where to adjust, how to adjust, and knowing when not to adjust is very important. If we lose that to another group, we would not benefit humanity as much as we do.

Chiropractors should be chiropractors and that is the imperative. We want to urge the general public that when they go to a chiropractor, make sure he is doing chiropractic and not doing a lot of other things. There's nothing wrong with exercises, there's nothing wrong with nutrition, but make sure the real reason the chiropractor is in the profession is to remove that interference to allow you to live a good, healthy, strong life. Chiropractors are the only experts in the prevention and removal of subluxation.

Wright

Will you give our readers a couple of tips or some advice on how to stay out of doctors' offices and even stay out of chiropractors' offices? What can we do to make ourselves healthier?

Curzie

About 70 percent of what we see is stress related. When you are doing Yoga and you have a positive mental attitude, sure you're going to be a healthier being. When your body becomes run down and you are not able to function properly it is usually due to stress. In order to stay out of doctors' offices you need to eat healthy and you need to exercise.

Here in Alaska not everyone is outside all day long during the cold winter months and we need to make sure we are doing some kind of exercise, which will also help encourage a positive mental attitude. To stay out of a chiropractor's office (I'm not sure that's a good thing), you need to make sure you eat healthy, decrease stress, and have a positive mental attitude. You also need to be subluxation free.

Think about how many people there are who have written books on how to think positive and how to have a better attitude. These books focus on how to heal yourself from within. The future of health-care is going toward that. Sometimes we are not able to do that and that is where the chiropractor can come in to make sure your body is free of interference.

You see little kids and wonder why they are so cranky and have so many physical problems. They may have fallen down and received interference to their nervous system. It's amazing how different they are from start to finish when they have had chiropractic care. We should all strive to live like children.

Wright

What an interesting conversation. I really do appreciate your taking all this time with me to answer all these questions. I've learned a lot and I really do thank you.

Curzie

It's been very enjoyable. Thank you.

Wright

Today we've been talking with Todd E. Curzie, DC, LCP, DPhCS, who is talking about something that is on the minds of every person I know and that is healthcare. I think we've learned a lot from him here, at least I have.

Todd, thank you so much for spending so much time with us today on *Dynamic Health.*

About the Author

DR. TODD E. CURZIE received a Bachelor's degree in Biology from LaSalle University in Philadelphia, Pennsylvania, in 1991. He pursued his desire to become a Chiropractor by obtaining his Doctorate in Chiropractic in 1995 from the fountainhead of Chiropractic: Palmer College of Chiropractic in Davenport Iowa. In 2000, he received the LCP degree (Legion of Chiropractic Philosophers). His deep-seated passion for Chiropractic grew ever stronger and underwent a four-year study to become one of the first thirty-seven Chiropractors to receive a Diplomate in Philosophical Chiropractic Standards (DPhCS) in 2005.

He was married in July 2002 to Renee and has a beautiful son named Cooper William Curzie. Renee is currently pregnant with their second child.

He has been in active practice in Anchorage Alaska for the past eleven years. Dr. Curzie has a dynamic practice with the focus on the removal of the subluxation. Curzie Chiropractic has a large pediatric patient base. From very young to the very "mature in years," Curzie Chiropractic promotes health for all ages.

Todd E. Curzie, DC, LCP, DPhCS
Curzie Chiropractic
3210 Denali St., Suite 1
Anchorage, AK 99503
Phone: 907.569.9355
Fax: 907.644.8455
E-mail: drcurzie@alaska.com
www.curziechiropractic.com

Chapter 4

CAROLYN FINCH, MS, SLP

David Wright (Wright)

Today we're talking with Carolyn Finch, MS, SLP. She is an author, keynote speaker, and expert on body language and the brain-body connection. She is a consultant to government, industry, and media on body language. Carolyn energizes individuals and businesses to increase skills, change attitudes, and modify behavior to improve health, performance, and success. She is author of *Universal Handtalk: A Survival Sign System* and coauthor of *The Wellness Path.*

Carolyn, welcome *to Dynamic Health.*

Carolyn Finch (Finch)

Thank you, David.

Wright

So, how do you define "Body Language"?

Finch

"Body language" is a movement of the body as determined by four energies. There is electrical energy flowing through our entire body.

How to channel and where the blocks are determines an individual's body language. One level is mental energy—thinking subconsciously, consciously, the unconscious state when we are asleep or under anesthesia or in a coma. The emotional state centers around the heart or in the areas in line with the heart such as the arm. This incorporates feelings and emotions such as hugging or pushing away with the hands. Body language is shown in the shoulders, arms, and chest movements. The third level of body language is the actual physical movement. The majority of the physicality of our body is in the waist, which is the center of the body. The movement of the hips determines a lot of what's going to happen in our bodies.

If you see a dancer or a couple dancing—totally integrated—you can see how much the energy from one person affects another. The environment in which the individual has been brought up in—family mores, nationality, and religious training and beliefs—often control this area.

The waist area or mid-torso connects the emotions and the physical base of the body. The hips determine how a person will walk and move. Since the hips also include the physical areas of love, sex, and growth, much can be determined by observation.

The fourth area is the spiritual growth and the spiritual energy represented by the feet. It is the feet that help the individual move forward, get involved, stand, follow, or lead. The feet are also the base to the spirit of the body. Witness any "Give me an A!" cheerleader and the spirit follows.

Wright

What would you say is your greatest contribution to the area of body language?

Finch

I believe my greatest contribution is in teaching others how to read Body Language to improve their health, performance and success. I have learned this myself through research, observation, and personal experience. I was a child with learning challenges. I had double vision and thick, "Coke bottle" glasses. I had difficulty learning to read. I was also what is known today as "hyperactive" and I always had a mind of my own.

In my age bracket most individuals are complaining about having to wear glasses. I started my eye training activities a half century ago and I heard my doctor say, "If she continues her eye exercises she won't have to wear glasses as an adult." Seeing the doctor stand there and tell my mother that news gave me the energy I needed to balance myself. I threw my glasses away thirty years ago and haven't worn them since.

Wright

I remember a really wise man telling me one time that if I happened to be walking down the road and saw a turtle sitting on top of a fence post, I could bet he didn't get up there by himself. Will you name some people who have been among your greatest assets?

Finch

If one were to call parents assets, that would be my answer. I was fortunate to have been brought up in a middle class environment by parents who cared about me and how I could function as a human being, even though they knew something was different—my eyes went off to the side and I also had to have braces for almost eight years. Almost every tooth in my mouth was moved. My parents always worked to help me improve. They scheduled everything for me—I had eye training time, piano practice time, and study time. My rewards were to go outside—nothing pleased me more than playing in the dirt, building huts, climbing trees, not typical girl things; but that's what I enjoyed. I honestly don't remember receiving many materialistic rewards. If I did, I didn't know they were major rewards and I certainly didn't ask for them. I believe my parents were always coaching me.

Most of the time I didn't realize what was going on. For instance, my dad brought me a picture of the horse Seabiscuit. He hung it up in my room and said, "This horse was small and had lots of challenges and if this horse could do it, you can do it—you can win."

So I do believe my parents have been my base assets. I doubt that I would have gotten through my teen years if I hadn't had that strong energy from my parents. The other adults were my four grandparents and my 4-H leaders.

Wright

I've never heard of eye exercises. You alluded to your eyes going off to the side, was that a muscle problem and did you have to strengthen your muscles?

Finch

Yes. There are six muscles on each eye. When the muscles are not functioning properly, there's a change in vision and the individual could become nearsighted or farsighted. Glasses can be worn to help the problem or vision can be corrected. Eye training is over one hundred years old and it's now coming into fashion. You can hear ads on television, radio, and you can speak with many different people who have used this before and after surgery.

Wright

Why aren't more people in touch with their bodies?

Finch

I believe people are not in touch with their bodies because we have been brought up to think of the body as a machine. Machines are cold, structured, action directed things that take raw materials and "spit out" a product. Our educational system, military, and health care has all been directed this way. Our medical field teaches doctors that the body has various systems and therefore it runs like a machine. If you have a problem you go to the elbow doctor, or nose doctor, or the toe doctor. We've segregated the body into parts rather than treating it as a whole. If something goes wrong, the attitude is it can be removed, replaced, or medicated similar to the manufacturing system. Therefore, feelings, emotions, and spirit have not really been taught or experienced by most individuals. Also, we have not been given permission to take care of ourselves. Advertising and culture has instructed us to "go" to the doctor or professional for every little thing. I grew up in a time when no one mentioned the word cancer. Even though I grew up in a cancer cluster and many of my neighbors were dying, the disease was not mentioned. It was just considered "the big C" and nobody discussed it.

I feel that most people today are living in a fight, flight, or freeze state most of their lives. Fight, flight, or freeze are the basic characteristics of a piece of machinery. It goes haywire, a part breaks or it jams. And comparing the body to a machine is the base of stress and the base of disease. When individuals begin to function as whole beings connected to the Universe, then they develop a balance of mental, emotional, physical, and spiritual uniqueness of self.

Wright

I know that there are volumes and volumes written on body language and that it's a large area, but would you tell our readers some basics on reading body language?

Finch

Sure. Body reading is something we all do—we're all generalists. Because there is so much negative thinking, individuals tend to distort much of what they see if they don't know what they're looking at.

There are however, four personality types that were discovered by Hippocrates many years ago. He knew who would get sick and what kind of diseases they would get.

I've had a background in the Speech Pathology field of medicine for several decades. In Speech Pathology, we work with swallowing and choking disorders in hospitals and health care centers. Most lifestyle diseases end in speech, swallowing, and/or choking disorders. There is dramatic change in the language of the body as individuals in a family develop their diseases and seldom do professionals look at the personality styles and the body as a whole but more as a group of symptoms that can be addressed individually. Research shows that it takes ten to fifteen years for a disease to develop. And all this time whole body movements can be observed to be out of balance. There are constant changes in facial expression—more frowning, eye squinting, and coughing—during eating. In the upper body there are changes in breathing, noticeable shoulder imbalances down to inappropriate posturing and walking. There is constant change in the body language. We know that personality style as well as growth and development have a lot to do with the way the person appears, however, we are not educated to work with personality styles and how they learn and function. There are many more than four styles but this is a good place to start.

The four basic personality styles have been translated into:

1. The analytic,
2. The driver,
3. The amiable, and
4. The expressive.

The analytics are usually busy analyzing things. The drivers work toward end results. The amiable changes his or her mind, yet acts as the "team cheerleader." The expressive usually likes bright colors and takes risks without being concerned about end results.

Analytics tend to keep their arms fairly close to their body in most of their movements. The drivers have their hands out in front of them usually doing an activity. The amiables may fold their arms or hands because it's a comfortable position for them. The expressives are usually waving their arms around while they're talking. This is very basic

Those would be some basics that people see every day.

Wright

How important is it to talk to children?

Finch

Based on the observation of their body language, it's very important to talk to children about what is seen. It's important to know how a person is developing because this is what we see as adults.

I'll give you an example of a two-year-old. A two-year-old might want to wear the same shirt for days, night and day, if he or she could. I salute the parents who let the child be a bee or love the fire truck shirt so much that they want to keep it on for days. Time means nothing to two-year-olds. They're just like little scientists, experimenting in this great laboratory of life. As a matter of fact, this is a great time for bartering with the child: "If you act in an unpleasant way, the shirt comes off." The child will outgrow this phase and develop some really good decision-making skills and feel good about himself or herself.

If we see children of different ages acting like a two-year-old, perhaps they've skipped the developmental needs for that age, or maybe they were even stifled. Perhaps they weren't permitted to leave their outfit on for a few days making them feel good and helping with their self-image, so therefore, as they grow through life, they may be making up for things that they were unable to experience at two, or three, or four, etc. These "body language leads," as I call them, help adults when they have a discussion with a child. Ask questions such as, "How do you feel when your hair is like that?" "How do you feel when you wear that shirt?" "How do you feel when you wear that necklace?" Many times we criticize rather than find out how the person feels. Once we ask about feelings, we can elicit much more conversation from an individual.

While asking children questions it is important to observe their body language while the two of you are communicating. One of my speeches is titled: "What is your Child's Body Language Saying About You?" So notice closely what messages your child is sending.

Wright

Why is body language an important tool?

Finch

Our body language helps us have a great performance. This is not just for actors, musicians, or politicians but it's for anyone who faces another person on a daily basis. When a person faces another person, it's really about the other person, not always about ourselves. Yet, we can see a person standing there, waiting for us to finish talking so that he or she can talk. When we stand erect, we can breathe more easily, we're prepared to receive information from the other person, and we can speak with more eloquence. When we close off another person we're blocking out customers and friendly conversational exchange.

If we know a lot about the basic personalities as I mentioned, we can determine the ones who will resonate with our vibration. If the vibration is negative and lacks synchronization, then we may wish to do business with someone else or do business elsewhere. If we're not interacting with a family member, then perhaps a person is stuck with one personality and hasn't grown in all four ways.

The fifth personality is a combination of all four personalities. This balanced adult can get along with anyone because he or she knows so much about body language through what they have experienced within themselves. Without realizing it they have learned so much about the four personalities that they're able to communicate with any one of them at any given time without frustration.

Wright

Tell me, why did you choose body language as your main theme?

Finch

I chose body language as a main topic for writing and speaking because I have accumulated experience over the years. This has been my focus for most of my keynote speeches and seminars. I've been a Speech Pathologist for forty-six years. Twenty of those years I've been a Nutritionist, a Reflexologist, and an Applied Kinesiologist. Kinesiology is the study of the movement of the muscles of the body. All of these areas address the way the body functions. The last three areas I mentioned—Nutrition, Reflexology and Applied Kinesiology—are all adjuncts to my earlier jobs as an actress, model, and as a college professor teaching verbal and non-verbal communication.

The knowledge I have of the human body is from years of experience and lots of research and development of ideas and what is already out in the marketplace. I'm author of *Universal Handtalk: A Survival Sign System,* which is the result of my research and experience with accident, stroke, and comatose patients over a period of ten years. We use Universal Handtalk in hospitals with firefighters, EMTs, and others so they can communicate with foreign-speaking people and with individuals who cannot speak due to fear or those who are challenged.

I feel all this is a good base for what I'm now speaking and writing about.

My research, writing and speaking continues because I am passionate about individuals learning more about themselves for themselves rather than always pleasing others. I also feel individuals need to learn to get in touch with who they are through many alternatives.

Wright

I was so taken with a speaker once at a seminar. His Kinesiology experiments were so fascinating that I checked out some books on the subject. I found it truly fascinating how the body and mind interact. I still use some of what I learned today.

Finch

I feel it's being more accepted and as far as the Kinesiology is concerned, my new book, *A Victory at SEE—How to Read Body Language for Dynamic Health, Performance, and Success* tells a lot about Kinesiology and how people can actually test themselves and know where they are out of balance and what they can do to improve. We don't have to be as sick as we are. When there are imbalances in the system they can be corrected so the electrical energy can continue to flow thus diminishing or avoiding certain diseases.

Wright

The information you get from kinesiology is not only fascinating but once there is a belief level, it's just so simple to apply.

If I understand about the brain-body connection, are you saying that I will have better health and performance?

Finch

Definitely. We've heard so much about the left brain and the right brain but only recently has anybody really talked about the whole brain? I don't know about you, David, but I really don't want to be half-brained!

The one field that is of real importance in Kinesiology is a program called the "Brain Gym®." The program is Educational Kinesiology and it's helping educators, individuals, and families understand how to use the whole brain to get ready for learning, organizing, and focusing.

An example of that is: The left brain is like low gear on a car; but we need the left side in order to get started because that's where we have detail. The right brain lets us hit cruising speed so we can see the big picture. Most people live life from their left brain. In other words, they get started but it's very difficult for them to keep going. A person who is using their left brain when they're driving is looking at the car directly in front of them. The right brain thinker looks a little bit ahead because they're looking for the big picture. The whole brain driver sees the entire landscape. They see the close-up, they look a little farther, and then they look toward the horizon. They also see what's on the periphery. They can see the whole picture and they can switch back and forth any time they want—from the car in front, to the horizon, to the sides of the road, so they become safer people— healthier people—because they're using everything. The whole brain driver not only sees the entire landscape but they move very quickly from low gear to high gear and back again, whereas a person who's only focusing on one side of their brain is using perhaps low gear and then very slowly moves over into high gear.

Through the Brain Gym® and many other programs out there, we're able to work with children in particular who have challenges and we're able to move into being faster learners, quicker thinkers, and better readers. It's amazing what we can do when people get out of that left brain and start to be whole brain thinkers. This, of course, affects the balance and health of the whole body.

Wright

My problem with the right and left hemisphere is that it's so much fun to stay over in the right side isn't it?

Finch

Seeing the big picture from the right brain might be fun for you and me but for someone else it may be very scary. That may be one reason why some people don't take that step. As a Speech Pathologist—a person who deals with words—I can really listen to a person and hear whether or not he or she is in the left brain or right brain by the words being used. We can also tell by the way the eyes are functioning and the hands are moving.

Wright

I've heard people teach that 95 percent of all communication is non-verbal. It's strange that you would be a Speech Pathologist and be teaching body language now.

Finch

In the development of the individual, the hardest thing a person can do is to speak because all of the systems of the body have to be synchronized. I have worked with children from birth up to individuals who are 105 years old. In the process of working with all of these age groups I usually go back to activities from the first two years of life when a human being learns the most. Research tells us that 75 percent of what a person learns by the age of eighteen, they have learned by the age of six. That is the base as to why we have so many early childhood programs in our country and why we have government agencies for early intervention where professionals go into the home to help parents and caregivers immediately when the parent or physician notices a lag in development. This lag in development is noted in their child's Body Language. Unfortunately many school and educational institutions misinterpreted early learning and subject children to early academics. In reality, children learn through movement and when they are not given the opportunity to move their brain-body, coordination weakens. Some schools have done away with recess and many kindergartens no longer have outdoor play. Learning as much as we can about Body Language will help educators, health practitioners, and parents intervene and expose their children to developmental activates rather than brain drain activities. When children can move and the brain can develop appropriately many problems can be prevented

Body language has to be developed on both sides of the body and then in the center. From head to toe, the fun things in life are really in the middle of the body, therefore, we have to develop the whole middle of the body including what is called "core muscles" before a person can speak appropriately. Speech is the tip of the iceberg because it is an on and off form of communication. Body Language functions 100 percent of the time, even when sleeping. By knowing more about the movements of the body we can know more about which side of the brain is communicating to the body and understand the individual needs more appropriately.

Wright

Well, what an interesting conversation. I could go on for hours but obviously we're under some time constraints here.

I want to tell you how much I appreciate your answering all these questions and making this subject clear to me. I've really learned here today and I'm sure our readers will as well.

Finch

Thank you so much.

Wright

Today we have been talking with Carolyn Finch. She is an author, a keynote speaker, and expert, as we have just found out, on body language and the brain-body connection. She consults with the government, industry, and media on her topics. She energizes individuals in businesses in order to increase their skills, change their attitudes, and modify behavior to improve health, performance, and success.

Carolyn, thank you so much for being with us today on *Dynamic Health.*

Finch

You're welcome and thank you so much for having me.

About The Author

CAROLYN FINCH is a nationally recognized Body Language Expert, author, and motivational speaker who *helps* individuals and businesses increase skills, change attitudes, and modify behavior. She is a Speech/Language Pathologist, Applied Kinesiologist, and Nutritionist. Carolyn is author of *Universal Handtalk A Survival Sign System,* which is used in hospitals, with firefighters, EMTs and others where there is a speech/language barrier.

Her new book is *Victory at SEE, How to Read Body Language for Dynamic Health Performance and Success.*

Carolyn Finch. M.S. SLP
Electrific Solutions, Inc.
Phone: 203.775.0290
Phone: 800.864.1022
E-mail: carolynf@electrific.com
www.electrific.com

Chapter 5

DR. EARL MINDELL

THE INTERVIEW

David E. Wright (Wright)

Today we are talking with Dr. Earl Mindell. Like Drs. Spock, Edell, and Ornish, Dr. Earl Mindell has become a household name to millions of North Americans. When the *Earl Mindell's Vitamin Bible* exceeded seven million worldwide and published in thirty languages, he had become a phenomenon. Currently it has sold over ten million copies worldwide.

Some of Dr. Mindell's previous books include *Earl Mindell's Soy Miracle, Earl Mindell's Herb Bible, and Supplement Bible, Safe Eating, Food as Medicine,* and *Shaping Up with Vitamins.* He conducts nutritional seminars around the world and makes daily appearances on radio and television programs.

Dr. Mindell holds a Ph.D. in nutrition and is a professor of nutrition at Pacific Western University in Los Angeles. He is a California registered pharmacist and a master herbalist. He is a charter member of the American Academy of General Practice of Pharmacy as well as the American Pharmacists Association.

Dr. Mindell, welcome to *Dynamic Health.*

Dr. Earl Mindell (Mindell)

Well, it's a pleasure to be here. Actually I should add some of my other books too: *The Prescription Alternatives, The Diet Bible,* and *The Allergy Bible.* I have forty-seven books as of today and I'm working on a few more. I'm always working on more books.

Wright

I went to Amazon.com just to check your book titles a few days ago.

Mindell

It's a little embarrassing. On Amazon they have about ninety-five things. They are not all books; some are tapes etc., but they've got almost everything. Well, you know some are, of course, out of print now because I've been writing for more than twenty-five years.

Wright

Dr. Mindell, millions of people are taking vitamin supplements today. However, in a recent article in *Biography Magazine*, you were quoted as saying, "Vitamins are no substitute for eating well." So, how do vitamins help the body?

Mindell

Well, let me say this. It's pathetic that the United States—one of the richest nations in the world—is a third world country when it comes to nutrition. Vitamins don't replace a terrible diet, but boy, you sure do need supplementation because of this horrific diet we're eating. I call it the "standard American dieter's fad"—it's more like pathetic. I also call it the "Twinkie, Ding Dong, doughnuts, pizza, Prozac, Pepsi" diet.

Basically, vitamins work *with* food to produce energy. They are necessary for optimal health, which means your body is working as efficiently as possible, and for life as we know it. So it's important to get all the necessary nutrients. If you're lacking one vitamin it can cause a problem with the other ones as well.

Wright

In the same article, when asked about the secret to your success, you were quoted as saying, "I simply tell people the truth about how to take better care of themselves." From whom do people get erroneous information about their health?

Mindell

Well, they don't get *any* information about their health. They only get information about their sickness. I mean, all you have to do is watch commercial television any particular night and you are inundated with all these drug ads for sickness. You don't hear anything about health. You know we call it "health insurance," but it's not health insurance—it's sickness insurance. We only hear about what to do in case of sickness and what to do. No one tells about health or preventing sickness and keeping this incredible body healthy.

Life expectancy is about I guess about seventy-seven years on the average for male and female, doing what we do. If we were to be really educated about how to take care of ourselves, 100 would be the normal life expectancy.

Wright

When the first edition of your book, *The Vitamin Bible*, came out in 1979, the medical community scorned you. They said they thought you were a fanatic. In the past ten years, though, major research studies have changed—even the medical establishment's attitude. That must give you a tremendous satisfaction.

Mindell

Well, it does. In fact, *The Journal of the American Medical Association*, October 2002 edition came out with a research article stating exactly that—everyone should be taking a vitamin and mineral supplement.

As I mentioned I'm an antique collector. I have quite a collection of antique pharmacy and medical things. I have a book published in 1938 by the American Medical Association showing they were very big on vitamins back then! Of course, after the Second World War with the advent of the utilization of synthetic drugs like penicillin, etc., the drug companies said, "Let's dump all of these old remedies and just concentrate on these synthetic drugs." And boy, they've done a pretty good job in the last sixty years. So it's not a new concept, but because diet and lifestyle has changed so dramatically in this country, even the so-called "establishment" is becoming aware that there's no way you're going to get enough nutrients in your diet.

Wright

In 2002 the *Journal of American Medical Association* reversed their twenty-year-old stance against vitamins.

Mindell

Correct.

Wright

What affect did that have on the public's attitude towards adding vitamins to their diet?

Mindell

Well, I think it definitely helps when you have the so-called establishment saying that it's imperative people take a supplement. For instance, the March of Dimes (which is a pretty "establishment" charity) has ads going all over the place telling women of childbearing ages that they should be supplementing their diet with folic acid, one of the B vitamins. Lack of folic acid can cause incomplete development of the brain, spinal cord, and/or their protective coverings—a defect called spina bifida. A lack of folic acid, which just about everyone in the country has, causes the body to produce an over abundance of a toxic amino acid.

Amino acids are the building blocks of protein called homocystine and that is probably a greater contributor to heart disease than elevated cholesterol. By getting enough folic acid in the diet through supplementation, it will prevent homocystine from being produced. So you can see that we are learning our diet is probably responsible for, I would say, seventy-five to 85 percent of the problems we have.

Wright

Dr. Mindell, you have said that low-fat diets have made people fatter than ever. How can that be?

Mindell

Well, that's a good question. Five or ten years back we were told low-fat is the way to go and all of a sudden people started switching over to these low-fat or no-fat things. They didn't realize that the companies that produced foods would load them up with sugar and processed carbohydrates. So it's pretty evident that no-fat or low-fat is not the way to go.

I think we should decrease the amount of the processed carbohydrates and sugar; we're eating 150 pounds of sugar per person per year. To give you an idea how much sugar you're eating and don't even realize it, if you drink a typical twenty-ounce soft drink, you're getting fourteen teaspoons of sugar in that soft drink!

Wright

Wow! Goodness! The only diet supplement I've ever taken is one of these jumbo jobs every day that is time released. But the way I read your book, you almost have to take vitamins with food, right?

Mindell

Oh, absolutely. You should be taking a vitamin supplement *with* food. I take a pack in the morning with breakfast and then also with my evening meal. You don't time release your food, so why should you time release the supplements? You should be taking them at least twice a day. Theoretically, you should take them three times a day, but that is very impractical for the average person. If I could get people to take them twice a day, I'd be happy.

Wright

And what they do is they supplement what you're not getting?

Mindell

They supplement what you're *not* getting and they make sure you're getting enough of what you *should* be getting.

Wright

Let me read a quote from you, "Each year 140,000 Americans die from the adverse effects of prescription drug use and 938,000 Americans are injured due to prescription and dispensing errors. Eleven million people are abusing prescription drugs. Drug companies are forming alliances with HMOs to control the drugs you take, often at the expense of simpler, cheaper, and healthier lifestyle changes." Wow!

Mindell

Well, actually those statistics are a little bit out of date. It's about 140,000 Americans die from prescription drug use outside of hospitals and another 100,000 in hospitals. If you were to take the amount of people in the United States dying from prescription drugs, it's probably the fourth leading cause of death.

Wright

Wow!

Mindell

And it's getting worse. Let me tell you something, we are definitely subsidizing the world when it comes to the cost of drugs. We pay more than anywhere else in the world for prescriptions. Patients go to Canada, our neighbor to the north and are getting prescriptions filled there at half the price charged in the United States.

Wright

So how do we reverse this trend?

Mindell

Well, we start promoting wellness—you know, if you're well, you don't need prescription drugs. What a fantastic idea that is! I mean, we have our politicians running around the country saying we have to cut the price of prescription drugs for the elderly and they go on generic drugs. Well if they were healthy, they wouldn't need prescription drugs.

Wright

Dr. Mindell, it would seem that with all the research about the importance of good health, we are in a revolution. Where do you see the future of the wellness revolution?

Mindell

I see something that was talked about in the book that said, and I agree, that the wellness business—if you want to call it that—is going to become bigger than the sickness business. It will be a more than one-trillion-dollar business because people are living longer. People want a better quality of life and they want to be in good shape in the last years of their life. I mean, big deal—you live an extra year or two years longer if you're put away in a convalescent hospital or are connected to some machine. That's not what you want. We're much more informed of this whole thing now, and it *is* a wellness revolution. It's too expensive to continue what we've done before—wait until you get sick and try to pay to get well.

Wright

Just off the subject for a second, I was looking at one of the articles you wrote when you were one of the contributors in a magazine. It listed several vitamins starting at A and going through B_1, B_6, and D and C and all. I just started reading what these do. Vitamin A, for example—if I read correctly here—the benefits are that it is essential to eye health and builds resistance to respiratory infections.

Mindell
Right.

Wright
It boosts the immune system, promotes strong bones, healthy skin, hair, teeth, and gums.

Mindell
Right.

Wright
So why in the world—?

Mindell
Well, you know, you said we're probably contemporaries when it comes to age. I remember when I was a little boy (I grew up in western Canada—a very cold climate) my mother would give us a spoon of fish liver oil in the winter. I think we would run to school faster because it tasted so horrible. Fish liver oil is a good source of vitamin A and D. In a cold climate, you're not outside very much, and you don't get the sun as much, so a vitamin D supplement was important. Vitamin A is an anti-infective vitamin, and yet today people don't know about it. Today we don't give our children fish oil or whatever—we give them antibiotics. So maybe people knew something back then that we have ignored.

Wright
Let's change the subject for just a minute. What do you think of the Surgeon General's report on obesity in the United States?

Mindell
It's about time! I'm glad that the Surgeon General now calls obesity and overweight a disease. (Actually it was the last Surgeon General.) He has stated that 300,000 Americans die every year from the complications of obesity such as heart disease, diabetes, hardening of the arteries, high blood pressure, strokes, and how about this one: If we could get people's weight back to normal (two out of three Americans are overweight), and if the average American was at an

average normal weight, 40 percent of the cancers we are afflicted with would not occur. *Forty! Four zero!* It's about time. In fact, some years ago, one of the national newspapers' headlines claimed one-third of Americans born in 2000 would get diabetes. It's pretty frightening to think that we're bringing up a generation where a third of the children are diabetic.

Wright

Goodness! You know, as I looked at all the information about vitamins, I ran across the definition of minerals. Now, do you mix the two or are they mutually exclusive or what? For example, I was interested in this one (I guess it's called selenium). It acts as an antioxidant, which I really don't understand. It says it slows the aging process.

Mindell

Well, let me say this. I really should have called my book *The Vitamin/Mineral Bible*, but minerals are the "Cinderella" of the nutrition world. They don't get the play that vitamins do, but they are as important—if not more important—than vitamins. You cannot make a single mineral in your body so the two, of course, work together.

The main thing to mention about selenium is that not only is it an antioxidant but it also has anti-cancer properties. It's found in things that people don't eat a lot of such as onions, garlic, brown rice, and seafood. It works along with vitamin E and other anti-oxidants to make it even more potent.

Here's the best way to describe what it does: There's the good guys and the bad guys. The good guys are called antioxidants, and the bad guys are called radical oxygen molecules that are increased by stress, by the things in diets that are called the "fat cats"—fat, alcohol, tobacco, sugar, and salt. They keep the radical oxygen molecules from being produced. Anyway, the bad guys speed up the aging process and lead to degenerative diseases such as heart disease, cancer, and stroke, etc. (We're not dying of old age—we're dying of degenerative diseases and I believe eighty or 85 percent of them can be prevented.) But you want to have more of the good guys in your body than the bad guys and selenium, vitamin E, the carotenoids, vitamin C, and things such as green tea, grape seed, soy foods, and garlic are a very rich source of antioxidants. All these foods and nutrients help to neutralize the bad guys.

Isn't it pathetic though? You know, here's you are—I'm sure you are a well educated person—but you know so little about these health subjects. I'll bet you know which drug to take if you have a headache though.

Wright

You know it's embarrassing. I've spent half my life in some school or another, but my gosh! It's unbelievable how little I know.

Mindell

You know, there is such a need to really reeducate people about wellness, and I think it's going to happen only because of the financial situation. Once people start being really hit in their pocketbook—. I mean, anybody who has what I call "sickness insurance" (as opposed to health insurance) knows every year it keeps going up and up and up and there's no end to it. If you haven't had a prescription filled recently, the average prescription now is $65 on the way to $100. You say, "Oh I have a policy that I pay a co-payment." Well, watch out because that co-payment is going to be close to $25 to $50 very soon.

Wright

Right, and actually medical insurance in this country is so expensive that we don't take out medical insurance—we just make monthly payments on our medical bill.

Mindell

Exactly.

Wright

Even though you pay just a small portion of the co-pay, the other is indicated in your premium.

Mindell

Yeah, and then there's taxes too (you might have heard of those). So if we continue to do this—if we don't start focusing on wellness and prevention—we're going to bankrupt the country.

Wright

You know with our book, *Conversations on Health and Wellness*, we're trying to encourage our readers to be better, to live better, and be more fulfilled by listening to the examples of our guest authors. Is there anything or anyone in your life who has made a difference for you and who has helped you to become a better person?

Mindell

Well, absolutely. My mentors are many. I knew Dr. Linus Pauling, an amazing, brilliant scientist who studied the benefits of vitamin C, etc. Jack La Lanne has always been one of my heroes. Still in his upper eighties, he has been exercising forever. He says he still doesn't like to exercise but he does it anyway. I can go back to Robert Cummings, an actor that was into this in the twenties. I had the opportunity to meet the Shute brothers from London, Ontario, who were the first people who did the research on vitamin E. So it goes on and on, but I think the big thing I'd really try to tell people is that we have got to take as good care of ourselves as we do our dogs, cats, automobiles, and rose bushes, because if you really look at it, most people take better care of their cars than they do themselves. You hear these ads all the time: every 3,000 miles take your car in for an oil change, and make sure this is in order. People get their car washed on a regular basis. Well, how about our bodies? Why don't we know how to take care of them? I think when a baby is born we should get a maintenance manual. That probably would be a good idea.

Wright

Robert Cummings—boy, I tell you, that brings back great memories.

Mindell

He was a wonderful man.

Wright

He was young looking.

Mindell

He *is* young looking. He was into this back in the twenties and I had an opportunity of knowing him and learning from him. The health field is not new. It was probably started in the twenties. We're doubling our knowledge about nutrition every eighteen months, yet the average person is still in the dark and doesn't hear anything about this, and they really should.

Wright

I remember thirty or thirty-five years ago, I got involved in this company called Nutri-Bio that was some vitamin company, and Cummings was one of the—

Mindell

He was the spokesperson for that company.

Wright

Yes, and I'll tell you, he was taking vitamins daily. I mean morning, noon, and night.

Mindell

Well, guess what? I still am and I'm in my sixties now and I've been doing this for forty years. I'll tell you I get compliments all the time by people saying, "Yeah, you look fifteen to twenty years younger than you are."

Wright

If you could have a platform, Dr. Mindell, and tell our readers something that you feel would help them or encourage them, what would you say?

Mindell

I would say that if you want to be healthy, you have got to take responsibility for your health in your own hands. It's as simple as that. If you want to be sick, don't worry about a thing—it's going to happen. They are waiting for you at $3,000.00 a day. They have got a nice hospital bed and they are ready to come with the paramedics in the ambulance to pick you up.

Wright

Today we have been talking with Dr. Earl Mindell who has become a household name in the health and wellness industry. And as we have found out today, he probably knows as much if not more about vitamins and minerals than any man who lives on this planet.

Dr. Mindell, I really appreciate the time you have spent with me today.

Mindell

Thank you and stay healthy!

About The Author

DR. EARL MINDELL, worldwide best selling author of the *Vitamin Bible* and dozens of other books, wants to teach you all he knows about health and nutrition. Through the use of herbs and vitamins, Dr. Mindell's exclusive nutrition formulations have helped perhaps millions people lose weight, look younger, and feel better.

A pioneer in soy and many other nutrition and health breakthroughs, Dr. Mindell shows how to lose weight through his weight loss formulations and simple yet effective lifestyle changes. He also shares how to stay healthier and live longer. Join the nutrition revolution today and feel better through better health.

Visit and participate on his health and nutrition related message boards and visit his new bookstore where he has exclusive Earl Mindell specials. Don't forget to request a free product sample and/or a free newsletter while you are there and to check back often. The Web site is always being updated with new information and the latest news from Dr. Mindell.

Dr. Earl Mindell
www.DrEarlMindell.com

Chapter 6

BRYAN JOSEPH

THE INTERVIEW

David Wright (Wright)
Today we are talking with Dr. Bryan Joseph. Dr. Joseph is a caring doctor of chiropractic. About two years ago, he went through a life changing experience that positively altered his outlook towards his patients. He suffered from a rare sports injury, which is very difficult to diagnose. He tore ligaments along his pelvic floor, more commonly known as a "sports hernia." To make a long story short, he had a very sharp pain in his groin area every time he used his legs or moved his torso.

In looking for an accurate diagnosis he went to medical doctors several times, including: a urologist, a surgeon, a physical therapist, and a couple of chiropractors with very little success. Suffering with this injury for more than a year, he became frustrated and depressed and began thinking there was not an answer to his problem. However, this experience challenged his own clinical skills and changed his outlook toward treating and caring for others in pain. He now understands that pain is real and it can affect one's life.

After longing for a solution, his continued research helped him find a cure that restored his focus and gave him a new found purpose.

Dr. Joseph's purpose is to get people well and teach them how to stay there.

Dr. Joseph welcome to *Dynamic Health.*

Dr. Bryan Joseph (Joseph)

Thank you very much. It is a pleasure to be a part of this program and offer any advice I can.

Wright

What got you into the chiropractic profession?

Joseph

I really don't have a great story or anything that specifically triggered my choice of that profession. However, playing sports throughout my life I became extremely aware of the importance of a balanced body. I played football, baseball and basketball for years. When you're really active and your body is not physically balanced, or when body parts are not working the way you know they should, you become aware of it quickly because it affects your performance. So, due to my own increased body awareness I began to look for the right profession to help others perform at their best. Chiropractic came to the top of the list when trying to balance the body naturally.

Wright

Have you had any personal experiences that have helped you become a more passionate health care provider?

Joseph

Actually yes, I believe I have. I grew up around others who struggled off and on with pain. I always thought pain was a figment of the imagination. When I was playing sports I never really had any pain. But it wasn't until I actually experienced pain myself that I knew it was real. Knowing that pain is real and that the world was not just filled with tons of hypochondriacs, I started to understand what many feelings others were going through. My own pain was causing me to stop playing sports and forcing me to become sedentary. I hated this and slowly became depressed because of it. Looking back at my year-long experience of intense pain I can say it taught me to be a more passionate and caring doctor. Seeing things from the patients' perspective as well as knowing how badly I was affected has further pushed me to try and find the answer for everyone's pain.

Wright

Just as a side note, I have always heard the expression indicating people have either a high or a low tolerance—or threshold—for pain is that true?

Joseph

That is true. But research is telling us now that your diet plays a large role in your tolerance to pain. We now know the more bad fats we have in our diet the more inflammation our body will produce. There is a direct correlation between the amount of inflammation in our bodies and how sensitive we are to pain. Certain foods will produce more acidity or inflammation in our bodies causing us to become hypersensitive, therefore lowering our tolerance to pain.

Wright

What type of problems do you believe chiropractic is the most successful in treating?

Joseph

The word "chiropractic" is so often linked to back pain. We do have great success in the treatment of back pain and headaches; however, in my opinion chiropractic is a lifestyle change and is most successful when understood that way. Headaches, carpel tunnel, neck, and low back pain are some of the symptoms we work with routinely and obtain great results. However, we are most successful in helping people achieve true optimal health by looking at all the facets of their health. Nutrition, proper exercise, positive attitude, spinal alignment, and rehabilitation all have to be considered in order to reach optimal health. If everyone looked at the chiropractic lifestyle properly and understood the message of overall health then the greatest success would be the reduction of illnesses and the increase of many well-balanced individuals.

Wright

That is a great point.

Joseph

Thank you.

Wright

The last time I went to a chiropractor was about a year ago. I had numbness in my arm and he told me this is going to require some work on my part. He did a lot of things, but he also taught me some exercises and I would stand in the shower and do them. I have more movement in my neck now. I feel like my head's on a swivel; but those things he taught me sure did help and no more pain or numbness has ever returned.

Joseph

That's excellent!

Wright

We hear you are big on a team approach to health care. What other members of the team are important?

Joseph

I think the problem with our healthcare system today is we are chopping the body into so many different pieces. Everyone is specializing in one little area of the body and not looking at the body as a whole anymore. With this being the case we must take a team approach and piece-by-piece study the body parts until we fully understand the whole. Health care providers must look at the whole body.

You have to know your role in health care. You also have to know that there are other professionals who can work with you to make a patient's results that much better. I have always tried to look at the body as a whole, but when someone is not responding the way I expect them to, I find the right specialist to refer them to. As a chiropractor, for instance, we can't only look at the backbones when we know there are muscles and ligaments around it. So having a massage therapist and a physical therapist to do muscle work and rehabilitation is extremely important.

Our bodies must also be chemically balanced to be healthy, so I think someone doing nutritional work would be a strong asset to the team. Another member I'd have on my team would be an athletic trainer to teach proper movement patterns and home exercises for injury prevention.

Lastly, because I know the mind is a huge factor in healing, another member of my team would be a mental coach to help achieve individual goals through a positive mental attitude.

Wright

I was just wondering how you feel about the all the information coming out now having to do with holistic healing. Many people are writing and saying that if mind, body, and spirit are not all in alignment then we have trouble. Is there any truth to that?

Joseph

I would agree with that 100 percent. Growing up in a pretty medical orientated family I had a hard time understanding this. If someone would have told me that the body had energy and our attitude or mind frame made a difference in how we heal I would have thought they were nuts. I now know that being out of balance in any aspect will make a difference in your health.

Take a look at the types of healing that have been used the longest such as Chinese herbal medications and acupuncture. These techniques have been continually used throughout the years although technology has advanced. The reason they are still being used is because they are natural, safe, and effective. These healing arts are based on the holistic approach—looking at the body as a whole and now just treating symptoms. Results speak louder than anything else; therefore it's becoming more clear that we must address the mind and the body. I am confident in saying that to achieve maximum results, physical, chemical, and emotional balance need to be considered.

Wright

Well, I wouldn't want to embarrass you and I certainly don't want you to connect me with this next question but I do think we have to delve into it. Why do you think the chiropractic profession has a negative connotation associated with it?

Joseph

That is a really good question and I think it goes back to what I just mentioned about the various specialties that exist and really understanding what your scope of practice is. Unfortunately in any profession, including chiropractic, there are good and bad. A few bad apples can really stir the pot. Some professionals don't stay within their scope of practice.

In my opinion, the most negative connotations come from the fact that our culture has become conditioned through fear to focus on illnesses. Not until recently have we seen more people wanting to prevent illnesses or live a life about wellness and that is where the chiropractic lifestyle shines because we understand it and teach it.

Wright

What do you think is the cause of most people's back pain?

Joseph

The cause as I see it is two-fold—trauma and muscular deconditioning.

The age of technology is upon us and has changed how we use our bodies in our daily routines. I'm sure it would be safe to admit that you have used your body a lot less as you aged. It is so easy to sit in front of a television without ever having to get up in the evenings because of the remote control. Better yet, think about all the jobs that put you in front of a computer all day. We are just not using our muscles nearly as much as our ancestors did. Because of the lack of use, our muscles are becoming deconditioned or weak. The small muscles in the body that are designed to stabilize and support it and keep it balanced are becoming so weak that we have a hard time holding ourselves up. Therefore, our postures are changing and we are prone to injury and weakness because of the additional physical stress on our body. I believe much of the back problems that exist have come from our muscles weakening. There are exceptions when strong individuals suffer trauma leaving them with weakness in the ligaments of their back. A car accident is a good example. Emotional and chemical stress will also cause back pain.

Wright

Do you think walking might help that?

Joseph

I think walking is an excellent place to start. It helps get you moving as well as recharges your mind.

Wright

You know, everyone says that you have to go to a chiropractor forever once you start. Why would they say that?

Joseph

When I first started chiropractic school I actually had that same question in mind. Why does the treatment take so long or what seemed to be forever? Now having a much better understanding of our healthcare model I know the answer. Our medical society does not focus on prevention, but rather the focus is primarily on treating symptoms of current illness. On the other hand, the chiropractic profession focuses on prevention and treatments for wellness.

Trying to get healthy and stay healthy is an ongoing process. I have come to the conclusion there is no form of treatment that can make you healthy in one treatment. You might become pain free, but does that really mean you are healthy or cured? Continually addressing imbalances in your body, diet, and frame of mind is how you work on staying healthy. Your medical doctor never gives you a prescription for one pill. Lots of stressors, whether they are chemical, physical, or emotional, interfere with our overall wellness or health. So, the length of treatment to prevent illness and stay well should be ongoing for everyone. That does not mean you have to be treated forever, but you must put constant effort into improving your health.

I believe chiropractic is the best form of *health* care coaching that exists. Not only to stabilize or correct the spine physically, but also to help people be motivated to be healthier mentally and chemically. In my practice—and I would assume that every chiropractor's practice is the same—I only make recommendations and the patients will ultimately choose if they want to continue or not. When most people see the benefits of what the chiropractic lifestyle can do for them and understand what being healthy feels like, they want to continue chiropractic care throughout their lives.

Wright

I remember the last time I went to a chiropractor when I was having neck and arm pain. I looked forward to it because I knew it was helping.

Joseph

I have always thought this to be interesting, any time you were sick and you had to take an antibiotic for instance, you never took just one pill. Our treatments are no different in the amount given. Our treatments are hands-on so we have to see the patient frequently to continue to administer the treatment. It can take time to restore function to the nervous system.

Wright

You spend a lot of time out of your office doing health fairs, lectures, and volunteer work. Why do you do that?

Joseph

I do that purely to help educate the public. To make a good decision about something you must be educated. If someone wants to be healthy they must know some of the options available to achieve health. We get bombarded with pharmaceutical commercials. The only way we can ever get the message out about natural health care is to get out there and pound the pavement to spread the word of what we do. Natural health care industries do not have near the amount of money to spend on advertising as do the pharmaceutical industries. So I spend as much time out of the office as I can to get the message out. I believe I am slightly limited by the walls of my office. I want to make a difference in as many people's health as I can and part of doing that is educating the public.

Wright

How do audiences receive that message?

Joseph

Every time I have given a lecture somewhere it is almost as if a light bulb is turned on in someone's head. Whenever I have given a lecture or taught a seminar I get question after question from people wondering how health care can seem so easy. They want to know why no one has explained this to them before. I think we have made our health care system too complex. Keep everything in balance as best as you can physically, chemically, and emotionally and you will have a much healthier life.

Wright

When we talked a few minutes ago about the chiropractic profession having a negative connotation, I can remember when a short time ago chiropractic care was not covered by insurance and now it is. Did that not lend a tremendous amount of respectability to the entire industry?

Joseph

Not only are insurance companies covering chiropractic, but throughout the country there are hospitals hiring chiropractors.

Health care givers in other professions are now wanting to be taught our natural methods of treatment. That would have never happened years ago. The only reason it is happening today is because of the results patients are getting from chiropractic care. By no means do I intend to downplay the importance of crisis care, but I do think it is over utilized. Everyone is looking for the magic pill—a quick cure—without putting in any work, when sometimes putting in some physical work and eating healthy is the only solution. A pill may change your body's chemistry, but what does it do physically or mentally? The many medications taken off the market recently because of adverse side effects have been an eye-opener to people causing them to seek new forms of treatments. More and more people are looking for a cure for their problems, not just a quick fix for their symptoms.

Wright
You know, I thought I was a pretty intelligent boy but I look at television now and I see these ads selling medicines I can't even pronounce. I used to own an advertising company so I know what goes into making these ads. I see these magnificent ads selling medicines but many times I don't even know what they are for. How can medicines be sold when the public doesn't even know what they are for?

Joseph
The funny thing is I have a couple of family members who are pharmacists. I have asked them many questions about certain medications. They told me something interesting. When someone is looking at an over-the-counter medication such as Tylenol the brand offers variations on the product such as Tylenol for the common headache, Tylenol for migraines, or Tylenol for a tension headache. I was told that the ingredients in all of the various forms of Tylenol are nearly identical—they are just marketed differently.

Wright
Marketing.

Joseph
Exactly! And the scary part about a lot of the medicines is the side effects that can occur. It's funny when you watch the drug commercials on television; if you listen closely to the end of a commercial for example, a stomach medication, it will include possible side effects such as stomach cramps, diarrhea, gas, and constipation. I mean, the

list goes on and on and that's what the medicine was supposed to be helping with. The pharmaceutical industry dumps billions of dollars into marketing and politics.

Wright

What do you think the largest misconception is about chiropractic?

Joseph

Unfortunately, there are misconceptions such as chiropractors can hurt you or even can kill you. Maybe in the past, chiropractic was a little more misunderstood, however, there are now well over forty techniques available now that they didn't have years ago.

Many of the techniques are extremely light force and as gentle as a massage. Technology has also created instrumentation to rebalance the body gently and effectively. So the largest misconception I would say is that it can hurt you. People are afraid of neck adjustments because of the Bruce Lee movies that were out during the past that show an actor snapping someone's neck and killing them. The incidents of injuries in chiropractic offices are less than 1 percent. Adverse effects of surgeries or medications have a much greater risk than an injury from an adjustment. It is amazing how that idea got out there. The cost of our malpractice insurance in comparison to other professionals is a good example of our safety.

Wright

Can you tell us a success story you have had with a patient?

Joseph

I have many success stories. Every day I am working on improving the overall health of my patients. I have many patients who had been suffering with daily headaches or migraines prior to my treatments and no longer have them.

Just a couple days ago I had a really neat situation with a young girl. She was just about sixteen years old and had sprained her ankle about two months ago. She was playing volleyball and her ankle had stayed swollen for a period of about two months. She had been to her medical doctor and had gotten x-rays. There was no fracture so she was given anti-inflammatories and told to ice and elevate the injured ankle to reduce the swelling. The level of pain in her ankle started to go away but the swelling was not. Her mother brought her in to see me about reducing the swelling. I'm a sports oriented chiropractor so

I treat a lot of joints aside from the back. I examined her foot and found that there were several joints in the foot and ankle that did not have proper movement, which was causing the fluid to build up around her ankle. I adjusted her foot and ankle one time and did just a little bit of therapy and gave her a stretch to do at home.

The next day her dad, who had little faith in chiropractic, was shocked at how much of the swelling had gone down overnight! His daughter's ankle had been swollen for more than two months and much of the swelling had been reduced after just one visit to my office. That case was pretty exciting for me to share because you don't hear much about chiropractic successful treatment other than back and neck pain. Many health conditions can be greatly improved with proper chiropractic care.

Wright

You know, sports medicine is one of the most fascinating topics. I grew up in the fifties and of course Mickey Mantle was my hero.

I went to the stadium one day to see him and I can always remember that moment. I suspect if he had sports medicine going for him, his career could have been long enough for others to share my same memory. He would still be playing.

Joseph

You're right. It's amazing how many professional athletes and teams have chiropractors on staff traveling with them to help with their overall performance.

Wright

Oh is that right?

Joseph

I'm currently going through a program to become a certified chiropractic sports physician. During the program I have had the opportunity to train with chiropractors from the 1988 Olympics, the LA Lakers chiropractor, the St. Louis Cardinal's, St. Louis Rams, PGA tour chiropractors and many more of the best in our profession. The growth in this profession right now is amazing. Finally everyone is beginning to realize that a balanced body is a healthy body and this is our focus as chiropractors.

Wright

Before we close, do you have any additional advice you can give our listeners and our readers on living a healthy life style so we won't have to always go to doctors?

Joseph

I believe having the right attitude does more healing for you than anything. Keep a positive attitude and a good outlook on life. Know that you are blessed in everything that you do and have. Being able to wake up and take a breath every day is a gift and we must remember that. This outlook can help you live a healthier and happier life more than anything else. Always practice keeping a smile on your face and keep working to develop a positive attitude. Remember, when you run into obstacles or health concerns, there are people out there looking to solve your health problems, so don't ever give up.

Wright

What a great conversation Dr. Joseph. I really appreciate the time you have spent with me today. I know you are busy in your practice and I really do appreciate your spending this time with me.

Joseph

No problem. I enjoy speaking about something I am so passionate about.

Wright

Today we have been talking with Dr. Bryan Joseph who is a doctor of chiropractic. Clearly Dr. Joseph understands pain and suffering from his own personal experiences. Now he uses that understanding to help others in pain. Knowing that pain is real and how it can affect your life mentally and physically, he works toward improving the overall lives of all his patients. He has a newly found purpose—to connect the world with wellness. Thank you so much Dr. Joseph for being with us today on *Dynamic Health.*

Joseph

Thank you very much for having me as part of such a wonderful project.

About The Author

DR. BRYAN JOSEPH is a graduate of the University of Iowa and Logan College of Chiropractic. After playing years of football, basketball, and baseball he has developed not only a passion for sports, but a passion for improving the performance of athletes. He is a candidate to become a Certified Chiropractic Sports Physician, training under the chiropractors for the U.S. Olympics, the PGA tour, the St. Louis Rams, and the California Angels. Dr. Joseph specializes in functional rehabilitation, core strength training, and whole body improvement. Dr. Joseph is a very compassionate doctor who believes to truly achieve wellness one has to be emotionally, chemically, and physically balanced. Dr. Joseph feels everyone has room for improvement and should be treated like a professional athlete.

Dr. Bryan Joseph
5001 N. University St.
Peoria, IL 61614
Phone: 309.693.2225
E-mail: b_joseph2000@yahoo.com

Chapter 7

DAVID MEE-LEE, M.D.

THE INTERVIEW

David Wright (Wright)

David Mee-Lee is a Board-certified psychiatrist and an addictions specialist. Over the past twenty-five years, he has acquired expertise in dual diagnosis (co-occurring substance use and mental disorders). Dr. Mee-Lee is not your usual psychiatrist. Just because he has had past academic affiliations with Harvard University, University of Hawaii, and the University of California doesn't mean he's snobby and obscure. He writes and speaks in down-to-earth, jargon-free language.

Dr. David Mee-Lee, welcome to *Dynamic Health.*

David Mee-Lee (Mee-Lee)

Thank you very much. It's a pleasure to be here.

Wright

Dr. Mee-Lee, what do you mean by "co-occurring disorders" or "dual diagnosis," as it is sometimes called in mental health and addiction treatment?

Mee-Lee

"Dual diagnosis" in mental health and addiction treatment, or the more prevalent term used these days is "co-occurring disorders," is referring to people who present with a mental health problem as well as a substance abuse problem. Strictly speaking, a person who has a dual diagnosis has a primary mental health diagnosis as well as a co-occurring primary substance abuse or dependence diagnosis. Frequently there are people with mental health symptoms who are using alcohol or other drugs as a way to try to cope with their mental health problem. Sometimes there are people who have an addiction problem who, as a result of their addiction and substance problem, have mental health symptoms like depression, anxiety, or mood swings.

Many people who present to clinicians or even just living in the community, have mental health and substance problems affecting them at the same time. But, strictly speaking, a person with dual diagnosis has been diagnosed with an independent mental health problem as well as an independent substance problem. Both disorders have to be treated as primary disorders that need treatment at the same time.

Wright

How common is dual diagnosis?

Mee-Lee

Well, it's pretty common. Substance abuse treatment programs have typically reported that 50 to 75 percent of their clients have co-occurring mental disorders.

On the other side, clinicians in mental health settings report that about 20 to 50 percent of their clients have a co-occurring substance abuse problem. In mental health treatment settings, substance abuse treatment settings, even in medical settings, there's a high proportion of people who have both a mental health and a substance abuse problem.

Wright

Why do so many people have mental health *and* substance abuse problems? I can understand mental illnesses like depression, bipolar disorder, schizophrenia, and panic disorders. Are alcoholism and drug abuse really illnesses?

Mee-Lee

Many people wonder whether alcoholism and drug abuse are ill-nesses because our society has put a stigma on those who have these problems. People think of people who have an alcohol or other drug problem as being weak willed; or just that they are not trying hard enough to stop or control themselves. If you think about people who have problems with overeating and obesity, they don't want to be overweight and yet it's very hard to decrease their weight. People who realize smoking is a problem have a problem quitting. Once the detrimental habit crosses the line into being out of control, it takes on the characteristics of an illness.

The reason people have substance abuse as well as mental health problems is that mental illness can itself cause people to use substances as a way of trying to cope with their mental health symptoms. For example, with depression you can have sleep problems. Sometimes people who drink themselves to sleep trying to take care of their insomnia get addicted.

It can also work the other way where people have a substance abuse problem and, when they begin having problems with addiction, it starts affecting their family and work and they can't sleep properly. This can create anxiety and depression because they're losing their job or their family. Mental health and substance abuse problems can become very mixed up together because one illness can cause the other, or they can happen together.

It's important to remember that alcoholism or drug abuse has a life of its own. It can have its own course of improvement if treated; and it can have its own course of deterioration if not treated, just as the same thing can happen in mental illness.

Wright

Let me ask you a chicken-and-egg question: Do substance abusers use because of some underlying mental health problem; or are their mental health problems caused by their addiction problem?

Mee-Lee

This is often an area of controversy because, in the old days of mental health training, we were often taught that substance abuse can't be treated as an illness of its own. People thought that the addiction problem was caused by people's low self-esteem, or conflicts over dealing with some past mental health problem, or that they simply don't take care of themselves. It was taught that addiction was a compulsive disorder that causes them to be out of control and that's why they abuse substances. In the old days then, some people thought that it was purely mental health problems that caused substance addiction. On the other side of the fence, you had people who said addiction causes the mental health problems not the other way round.

People who work in the addiction treatment field sometimes don't take seriously enough the fact that someone may be having mental health problems. They say, "Of course you're having anxiety and depression—you are drinking and drugging too much and losing your job and family."

Both sides of the fence need to realize that yes, indeed, someone can have a mental health problem *and* a substance problem that can co-occur.

Wright

Is low self-esteem a mental health problem?

Mee-Lee

Many people would think of that as more of a mental health *problem*—it might not be mental *illness*. A lot of people can have low self-esteem and function fairly well except that they may not be as assertive as they want to be. There are other people who have low self-esteem and it's gotten to the point where it's causing a lot of depression and a lot of dysfunction. They're not able to be as functional at work or in the community as they might like to be. Sometimes when people have low self-esteem, the way they cope with that is to use substances as a way of getting in with a crowd that is more accepting of them. It can cause substance problems even though it started out with low self-esteem. So sometimes underlying mental health problems can indeed cause substance problems.

Once you have a substance problem it takes on a life of its own and you have to take both problems seriously.

Wright

Should substance abusers with mental health problems take medication? Do Alcoholics Anonymous and other recovery support groups tell people not to take psychiatric medications?

Mee-Lee

There are some people in support groups like Alcoholics Anonymous who would say substance abusers shouldn't be "chewing their booze," in other words, they shouldn't be taking pills, merely switching from drinking to taking medications. That is not an accurate view. If a person indeed has a co-occurring mental health problem, they may need medication, not only to stabilize their mental health problem but also to help them with their substance addiction problem. If you have an unstable mental health problem, that can set you up for having an unstable addiction problem as well. Some of the old timers in Alcoholics Anonymous and other support groups say you shouldn't be seeing psychiatrists and mental health people and taking medication because that's just another drug.

There's a pamphlet written by physicians in Alcoholics Anonymous called the *AA Member—Medications and Other Drugs.* This is one of the approved publications from AA. What they say in the pamphlet is that if medication can help someone "alleviate or control other disabling physical and/or emotional problems," then medication is recommended for people even in AA to take. It will help them with their co-occurring mental health problem and help them to be stable so that they're not setting themselves up to go back to drinking.

However, people who are in AA who do have a substance problem shouldn't take any medication just because the doctor gave it to them. They should be wary of taking addicting medications like addictive pain narcotics, sleeping pills, or addictive tranquilizers. It isn't a matter of being able to take just any medication they're handed. They need to take responsibility to learn what medications will be more risky for them because of their addiction illness and what medications would be helpful for them to take for their psychiatric problem, if they have one.

Wright

If there's a lot more awareness about co-occurring disorders, do mental health professionals get taught about addiction and vice versa so they can treat dual diagnosis clients?

Mee-Lee

Unfortunately many people in mental health training do not get taught about addiction treatment and a lot of people in addiction treatment training don't get taught enough about mental health. When it comes to treating people who have a mental health and a substance problem, which can be a major proportion of clients, the people treating them put blinders on. The mental health clinicians don't see the substance problem and the substance abuse counselors don't see the mental health problem. Even though we are becoming increasingly aware of co-occurring disorders, there's still a lag time in the training of professionals who work with both disorders. This results in clients not getting the best integrated treatment they should have.

Wright

Why do you think mental health and addiction treatment professionals have such different viewpoints about medication and treatment of dual diagnosis clients such as in AA?

Mee-Lee

If you think about it, for a long time in the United States, health professionals—mental health professionals, psychiatrists, and other physicians—didn't take addiction seriously. In this country it was really up to self-help recovery groups like AA to be the only people to take substance abuse seriously and develop self-help and mutual help groups to support them. So, the addiction treatment field in the U.S. had its roots in a more self-help, less formal education experience rather than formal health education and professional training. In contrast, the mental health field had its origins in traditional education, with college educated people and professional schools.

In the past there has been a clash between the self-help system and the more clinical, professional training system. This is changing as both sides begin to talk with each other and learn from each other, and as training has gotten better for mental health and addiction treatment professionals. The very different viewpoints between mental health and addiction treatment professionals really comes from different origins in terms of the treatment system.

In addition to this, society has always had mixed feelings about substance abuse—from the period of prohibition of alcohol in the 1920s, to people being very stigmatized for drug addiction. That's changing somewhat now as celebrities come forward and talk about their own drug problems.

Wright

So what do you do if the client accepts that they have a mental illness but they don't think they have a substance abuse problem, or vice versa?

Mee-Lee

Many clients may agree that they have a mental illness but are not so sure they want to work on their substance problem. Or they think they have a problem with alcohol, but they don't think they have a marijuana problem. Or they think they have a depression problem, but not a substance problem. Sometimes some clients with co-occurring disorders don't even think they have a mental health problem *or* a substance problem and yet they are getting into trouble with the law, or at work, or with family members, or with child protection services.

What you have to do is to start where the person is. If a person comes to treatment, they may be coming because of a court order, or a family member told them they had to get into treatment, or an employer told them they had to get treatment or they would lose their job. They're coming to treatment not because they want to work on their mental health or substance problems but because they want to keep their job, or not go to jail, or keep their family, or get their kids back. That's fine—what you do is start where they are and tell them you will help them stay out of jail or keep their family. You ask, "What is getting you into trouble?" They may answer that they got arrested and when you ask why they were arrested, you find out that they were dealing drugs or that they have an anger problem. Then you can begin working with their mental health (e.g., anger problems) or substance problems. You will be working with them not from the point of view that this is what they primarily want to deal with, but because it's causing them to get in trouble at work, or with the law, or with their family, *and* because they want to keep their job, stay out of jail, or keep their marriage. You start at the door they open and where they let you in rather than telling them they have to work on a problem they don't think they have. Work on what they're there for and from that point move to how their substance use and their mental health problems have been shooting themselves in the foot, preventing them from getting what they really want.

Wright

What kind of treatment program is best for people with co-occurring disorders?

Mee-Lee

There's no one-treatment program or one model where you have to go. The best treatment program is one that's going to be individualized to meet each client's needs in the treatment—that will look at whether the person has a very severe mental illness along with the substance problem; or whether it is a more mild mental illness along with the substance problem? How severe is the substance problem? What kind of family intervention needs to be done? What kind of motivational work needs to be done? If you have a person who is not ready yet to embrace full change, you have to put your emphasis more on motivational techniques to encourage and creative incentives for them to change. Or, if there is someone who is ready to do whatever it takes, you may have to focus more on relapse prevention strategies and help them to not take the drug and how to prevent symptoms with their mental illness.

The best treatment program is one that has a broad array of mental health and addiction treatment services—one that has a mixture of staff who understands mental health as well as addiction treatment—they've been cross-trained. The program should have a variety of levels of care so that if someone needs acute stabilization in an intensive level of care like a hospital or in a residential program, they can get that. If they are doing well enough that they can be seen as an outpatient and that keeps them stable, then that's available too, so that people can use whatever level of service that meets their needs.

We're really talking about flexibility, a broad continuum of services, cross-trained staff who understand mental health and addiction, and a system that focuses on individualized treatment, not just plugging people into set programs.

Wright

Can people with dual diagnosis really get well and recover? What does recovery mean? Does that mean they're cured?

Mee-Lee

Yes, people can get well and recovery. But recovery doesn't necessarily mean they're cured when you're talking about a chronic illness—no more than if somebody had diabetes or hypertension or asthma. You're not going to be able to cure these kinds of illnesses, but you are going to be able to help the person live well with their illness. A person suffering from a mental illness as well as a substance problem won't be able to be cured in the sense that they will never have a mental health problem or substance problem again. They can recover, meaning they can live beyond just the symptoms of their diagnosis. They can have an identity beyond just the fact that they have alcoholism or a mental illness. They can have goals and aspirations and be empowered to have hope to change their life in terms of their relationships, in terms of productivity in the community, and reaching their dreams and aspirations. Recovery is more than just thinking of them as people who are not drinking and drugging or not psychotic or depressed.

Recovery really means stabilizing their mental health and substance problem, but then living and growing to have an identity beyond just their illness and their diagnostic label. Comparatively, recovery from a medical illness would mean that the person is not just a cancer victim or a diabetic, but they're a person who's living and functioning and doing well in their life. At the same time they're keeping their illness stabilized and under control.

Wright

What should families and communities know and understand about co-occurring disorders?

Mee-Lee

Families and communities should know that one in three adult Americans are affected by alcoholism. There are an estimated twenty-eight million children of alcoholics, and there are people with mental illness who are working alongside you at work. People should understand first that there's nothing bizarre or weird about family members or people in the community having substance problems and mental health issues as well.

The second thing families and communities should know is that if they notice somebody having a problem, help is available; treatment works if they can get people into treatment sooner. Just like it's hard to help a person with diabetes and hypertension—if their illness is not identified and if they don't get into treatment soon—bad things can happen. The same thing is true with co-occurring disorders—if the substance problem and a mental health problem is not identified and they don't get treatment the illnesses can only worsen. It's important to encourage families and communities to reach out and help them to get into treatment sooner rather than later. It's also important to educate families and communities so that they can know where to turn and what to do rather than just worrying. There is a lot that families can learn about so they can decrease their own stress. But when families understand mental illness and addiction, it also helps the person who does have the mental health and substance problem to actually get into treatment and to receive some early intervention sooner rather than later.

Wright

I can really see some devastating results from dual disorders. When you're trying to fight one and don't know about the other or vice versa, I can imagine how hard it is on your clients.

Mee-Lee

It's hard enough to recover from *one* illness, let alone two. Sometimes people have a medical illness in addition to that and so they have three. Certainly yes, it is difficult and it is a challenge. But with good, integrated treatments and well-trained staff who understand both mental health and addiction disorders working together with their families and communities who are not in the dark about dual diagnosis, a lot can be done to help them.

Wright

Let me ask you another question. Regarding the people who are seeking help for dependency like alcoholism, do the people helping them suggest they go to a medical doctor and see whether or not something else might be causing their dependency?

Mee-Lee

Yes. I think whenever anyone is assessed, especially people with addiction problems, you don't want to just assume they're using solely because they're out of control with their substances. Yes, they are out of control with their substances but it could be related to the fact that they have a co-occurring mental health problem not well stabilized, which is messing the substance use problem too. Or it could be that they have a co-occurring physical health problem, which is making it hard for them as well. For example, a person may have chronic pain and end up being hooked on narcotics because their pain isn't well managed. A doctor could help sort that out. But there are other things they have to consider: such as where a person is living and who their family is. If they are living in a community where there are all kinds of drugs around, that's going to make it harder compared with someone living in a community where there are no drug dealers around.

One of the cautions though is that unfortunately, many physicians have bad attitudes about substance problems just like the rest of society. Many weren't taught in medical school to see substance and addiction problems as an illness ready to be treated. They were taught about the complications of addiction—liver problems and central nervous system problems—but many physicians still don't know how to fully assess addiction and help a person. They would be good at identifying whether the substance problem is being caused by some medical illness or a mental health problem, perhaps.

Wright
What an interesting conversation. I am sure the people who will be reading this chapter are really going to get some good information about a timely problem that affects almost every family these days, doesn't it?

Mee-Lee
That's true.

Wright
I really appreciate your taking this time out from your busy schedule to have this conversation with me, Dr. Mee-Lee.

Mee-Lee
I'm happy to do that.

Wright
Today we've been talking with Dr. David Mee-Lee. What a strange thing co-occurring disorders is to the layperson such as myself. I want to suggest that our readers check with Dr. Mee-Lee and others about this disturbing problem.

Thank you so much, Dr. Mee-Lee, for being with us today on *Dynamic Health*.

About The Author

DR. DAVID MEE-LEE is a Board-certified psychiatrist and an addictions specialist. Over the past twenty-five years, he has acquired expertise in dual diagnosis (co-occurring substance use and mental disorders). Dr. Mee-Lee is not your usual psychiatrist. Just because he has had past academic affiliations with Harvard University, University of Hawaii, and the University of California doesn't mean he's snobby and obscure. He writes and speaks in down-to-earth, jargon-free language.

David Mee-Lee, M.D.
4228 Boxelder Place
Davis, CA 95616
Phone: 530.753.4300
Fax: 530.753.7500
Voice Mail: 916.715.5856
E-Mail: David@DMLMD.com
www.DMLMD.com

Chapter 8

BERNIE SIEGEL, M.D.

THE INTERVIEW

David E. Wright (Wright)
Today we are talking with Bernie Siegel, M.D. He was born in Brooklyn, New York, and has attended both Colgate University and Cornell University Medical College, graduating with honors. Dr. Siegel is a life-long member of Phi Beta Kappa and Alpha Omega Alpha. Bernie received his surgical training at Yale New Haven Hospital, West Haven Veterans Hospital, and the children's hospital in Pittsburgh.

Bernie and his wife, Bobbie, reside in Connecticut and have five children and six grandchildren. Together, they have coauthored several books and articles and are currently partners in teaching as well as life. They travel extensively through the United States sharing his experience and groundbreaking therapeutic techniques.

Dr. Siegel retired from general and pediatric surgery in 1989. Bernie is well known to many; he has touched lives all across America.

Dr. Siegel became an advocate for patient empowerment in 1978 when he began the Exceptional Cancer Patients program (ECaP). He firmly believes in a person's right to live fully and to die in peace. Bernie predicts that the role of consciousness, spirituality, non-local, and heart energy will be explored over the next decade as scientific subjects. He embraces the philosophy of living and dying, which is at the forefront of the medical ethics and spiritual issues of our era.

Dr. Siegel, welcome to *Dynamic Health*.

Dr. Bernie Siegel (Siegel)

Thank you David, I have one correction. We now have *eight* grandchildren!

Wright

That's good. You're going to have your own ball team pretty soon!

Dr. Siegel, I've heard and read the phrase "mind, body, and spirit" in connection with healing, but you refer to it as a science of mind, body, and spirit medicine. Are people in the medical fields really studying it as a science?

Siegel

I can't say necessarily it's always in the medical field because I always say medical information is not a medical education. We get a lot of technology, but it's not always about the people. Others, however, are getting into the field of what you might call psychobiology, and, to make it—you might say to unify it—you have to understand that consciousness is something that is fascinating in the sense that the brain doesn't create your thoughts. You have a thought, and the brain mediates what you have thought and when it does that, it changes the chemistry of your body. For most people, when they're having a bad day, they don't feel good; that's chemistry and messages literally going to the body and every cell in it.

Wright

That's fascinating.

Siegel

So, on Monday there are more heart attacks and suicides.

Wright

Really?

Siegel

If you keep an intent, giving yourself negative messages—you know, ones that really say to your body, "I don't like life and living"—

it will result in illnesses. This is not about blame or guilt, but again, it's about the body responding to spiritual issues, to mind issues, and what's going on.

Wright

That's incredible.

Siegel

A lawyer put it well, maybe to summarize it. He said, "While learning to think I almost forgot how to feel." So, if we live in our heads we're really going to ignore the heart wisdom. Proponents of Kabbalah (Jewish mysticism) talk about "*hochmah*," which is the head wisdom, and "*binah*," which is the heart wisdom. Too many of us live in our heads when we need to be focusing on what brings us happiness and what feels right.

To make this practical, what I have seen from years ago, if you were to learn you have six months or a year to live and you don't like where you're living and you hate your job, what do you do? You quit your job, move, start doing what you love to do, and a year later you're not dead.

Wright

You have extended your life?

Siegel

It's not an accident. And, this is what I've seen. In my book, *Prescriptions for Living*, I call it "living your chocolate ice cream." That's what one of our sons replied when I asked, "If you knew you'd be dead in fifteen minutes, what would you do?" He said, "I'd buy a quart of chocolate ice cream and eat it!" I have watched people live their chocolate ice cream and die in their nineties when I had operated on them for a cancer I couldn't remove.

Wright

Wow!

Siegel

"Where was it?" "Where did it go?" Well, they went home, and they lived their chocolate ice cream. That's how you combine mind, body, and spirit.

Wright

Several years ago I went through cancer with my wife. Now, she is a cancer survivor. We were at the University of Tennessee in a group there at the Wellness Center. Of course, they use your books like Bibles over there; that was the first time I came in contact with the work that you've been doing.

We thought that many of the people were dying, however, some of them are still living as if they just simply refused to give up.

Siegel

If you go back to the science, a quantum physicist said, "Desire and intention alter the physical world causing things to occur which would not normally occur if they were not desired." Now, they don't tell you that in the doctor's office. Do you know what I mean? You go in, and they say, "You'll be dead in six months." You say, "What if I don't want to die in six months?" Well, that doesn't matter.

Wright

It doesn't matter?

Siegel

But, if you said it to a quantum physicist, they'd say, "Go home and fight for your life." Now, whether you live four years or twenty-four, I can't predict, but I know you'll outlive the six months. People are not statistics.

Wright

Right.

Siegel

Because of that, you know one really important aspect of it. The other is that we, as physicians, need to see ourselves as coaches. If a patient comes in the word I always listen for is "inspiration." When people say, "I have an inspiration," or, "You inspire me," I say, "Okay, you're a talented performer; come on, I'll coach you and we're going to have some great results."

You have to understand—going back to the first question of mind, body, spirit—how do you change yourself? You act and perform as if you're the person you want to be. So, if I put you on the stage and give you a comedy, your body chemistry is enhanced by the joy of the performance. If I give you a tragedy, I can get you sick, putting you in the same play night after night, where you're having a loved one killed or murdered or whatever.

Every action you perform has its effect on your body. So, if you want to survive, act as if you're a survivor.

Wright

That makes sense.

Siegel

If you have the coaches, be they books, tapes, or people, you'll accomplish far more than someone else who isn't willing to come to rehearsal and practice and put in the effort.

Wright

I remember reading that in the *Prescriptions for Living* book your office sent me. The quote was, "One of the best ways to change is to act as if you're the person you want to become."

Siegel

You know, that sounds so simple. I mean, when I first heard that, I said, "I want to be a more loving human being."

An anthropologist friend of mine, Ashley Montagu said, "Then behave as if you were a loving human being."

"What do you mean?" I asked.

He really made it very practical. He replied, "If someone I loved walked in the room, how would I behave? I'd go and do it."

That really helped transform my life and relationships by demonstrating and acting that way.

Wright

Could you tell us a little bit about ECaP, the name of your therapy program? What kind of work are you doing there?

Siegel

Well, it's not a company in a sense. We call it ECaP, which stands for **E**xceptional **Ca**ncer **P**atients.

Wright

What a wonderful name.

Siegel

It's a name my wife came up with when I wrote a letter to one hundred patients with cancer and invited them to come to a meeting. I'm expecting five hundred people to show up, you know, the original recipients of my letter bringing everybody else they knew who had cancer; but fewer than a dozen women came. We realized that there's only a minority who are willing to participate. The rest are very much into guilt, blame, and shame, thinking, "What did I do wrong? If he tells me I can help myself get well, then maybe it's my fault I got sick," or even, "I don't want to get well, and I don't mind dying. My life is terrible."

So, my wife labeled the ones who wanted to participate in the program "exceptional." We began the organization in '78 when a patient said, "I need help living between office visits." That's why I sent that letter out—to help people live with their problems. So, it became ECaP. We have a Web site too if people are interested. It's www.ecap-online.org. People can chat with me, find out my schedule, books, tapes, and all kinds of things. They can also talk with other people with problems.

Wright

I hope people will go to your Web site.

Siegel

I started group therapy then, and I'm still doing it. These are inspiring people. I'm doing it for my sake as much as theirs. Every week I sit down with people who really are trying to live, and it inspires me and helps me get through the week.

Wright

That has to help *anyone* feel better.

Siegel

And, you know, I don't preach one thing and then live another. I'm trying to live what I preach.

Wright

You've also written that love heals and that love is vital to our survival. The thing you said about love that I found fascinating was it didn't really matter who loved you. Can you explain that?

Siegel

Well, number one, when we are acting out of love, two people are helped—the person we're loving as well as the person giving love.

If I said to you, "What do you do that makes you lose track of time? What do you love to do so much that when you're doing it hours go by and it feels like a few minutes?" When those moments are occurring, your body is in a different state, like in a trance, and it's healed. You don't have aches, pains, and diseases when you're acting out of love.

Consider too the various statements we make about love, such as "love is blind." What does that mean? It means you don't see faults in others. So again, relationships happen.

Something really struck me the other day. We have a lot of pets and animals. We have a rabbit that lives in the house, and there's a cat we adopted that had a very difficult childhood. When we do something for them, like comb their fur, or pull their ears, they don't growl, ready to tear us to pieces—they lick us.

Wright

That's right.

Siegel

That breaks my heart—they're giving me love when I am hurting them or frightening them. They might be wondering, "What's he going to do to me?" when I'm grooming them. And really, if they're hissing or growling, I realize they're showing me what "love thine enemy means." When you give love, it's hard to have an enemy. You obliterate your enemy.

So, as my anthropologist friend, Ashley Montagu, said love is most vital to survival.

Too many of us today, however, are brought up without it. A study conducted at Harvard revealed that if you ask a college student, "What were your parents like?" and if they say, "My parents were loving," thirty-five years later only one in four had suffered a major illness.

Wright

Interesting.

Siegel

If they said, "My parents were not loving," then thirty-five years later 98 percent would have suffered a major illness. So, again, self-esteem and self-worth is important. If a child is told, "There's something wrong with you," that's very different than telling the child, "I don't like what you did. I love you, but I don't like what you did."

When a child grows up with self-worth and self-esteem, it causes him or her to take care of himself or herself. I keep saying that information doesn't change people, you know, we need inspiration.

Wright

That *is* inspiration.

Siegel

You show me a smoker who thinks it's good for a person to smoke. See? So, if you ask people, if they know it's not good for them, why are they doing it? Ah-ha! That's a whole other issue. What are they looking for? What is the addiction about? So, whether it's overeating, smoking, alcohol, or drugs, I mean, what are they searching for that they never got in their life?

Wright

I see.

Siegel

And, this is what I see. What I say to people is, "Take as good care of yourself as you do your beloved pet and you won't have any problems." I know people who smoke outdoors to protect their cats and dogs from lung cancer and other problems. And, they don't say, "I stopped smoking," they say, "I smoke outdoors now because my cat isn't well."

Wright

I was really fascinated by something you said in your book. If you lift up a baby to show people in an audience, there are two responses, sighing and applause, but when you lift up an adult, that doesn't happen.

Siegel

Yes, if I speak in a high school, I'll bring a baby. It could be before any audience, you know, but it strikes the kids more. I hold the baby up in front of a thousand high school students and they say, "Oh aw, oh aw," and they're all saying, "It's so adorable." Then, when I take a student out of the front row and lift them up; everybody laughs, "Oh boy, is that funny." Then, I say to them, "Look, there are only fifteen to sixteen years between the two of you; what happened? Why were you once a gorgeous baby, and now you're laughing at yourself?" It is important to really make the kids look at that because, believe me, high school students are more into suicide than they are into love.

Wright

Surely not.

Siegel

And, that is sad. It has its tragic effect on them later in life. So, I really do tell people to get out their baby pictures and take a look at them. I try to communicate to them that they're a child of God—to feel that they are divine rather than to tell them don't do this, don't do that, it's not good for you, but to get them to love themselves so they then do what is good for them.

Wright

You have a chapter in *Prescriptions for Living* titled, "Affliction can be fun—why false hope is an oxymoron and how to hold your life together." You also talk about detached concern. What do you mean by that?

Siegel

Well, detached concern is something they try to teach you in medical school. If you get overly emotional, how will you be able to take care of people? Now, I can tell you that I have operated on our son, my sister, and my mother-in-law. It doesn't mean that I was hysterical caring for them; I could be rational but care. That's what I try to communicate, because if you try to show detached concern to your family, how do you do that? You detach and it doesn't feel like you're concerned.

Wright

That must be difficult.

Siegel

As a matter of fact, when you're sworn in as a doctor and take the American College of Surgeon's pledge, you say, "I will deal with my patients as I would wish to be dealt with." It doesn't say, "I will care for," it says "I will deal with." Well, that's what bothers me. I try to get across to physicians that you can be rational and care and you won't lose yourself over those emotions.

The phrase "false hope" fits in there too, because hope is not statistical. Statisticians with cancer do better than people who don't understand statistics. If a doctor says that you have a 10 percent chance of surviving, you may not like the statistics, but it doesn't say you will definitely be dead, or the average survival is for two years. That's average but somebody lives one, and somebody else lives four or five or twenty. You have to realize you're not a statistic and hope is never false. Hope is real. It isn't about statistics—it's about what helps motivate people to keep living.

I often find doctors take hope away by pounding away at people to be in touch with reality, "You're going to die from this!" Yes, and then they'll go home and die in a week, because they become so depressed, their immune system closes down. When you take hope away, they don't live.

Wright

Dr. Siegel, with our *Dynamic Health* book, we're trying to encourage people in our audience to be better, live better, and be more fulfilled by listening to the examples of our guests. Is there anything or anyone in your life who has made a difference for you and helped you become a better person?

Siegel

I had a very unusual upbringing. I had parents who loved me, I got along with God, and had no problems in school because I was very bright and skipped many times. I didn't have all the afflictions that many people grew up with. I'm sure many people will answer this saying, "Oh my third grade teacher, oh my!" or, "You know, uncle George, or somebody . . ." If your parents love you, you don't need all those other people.

I grew up with three important principles from my parents. (I call these my "mottoes to live by," because I have met people who have mottoes that they're dying by.) One was about choices. My mother would ask, "What would make you happy? Which one feels good to you?" It's not about selfishness but my mother would have me focus on those questions in order to answer questions like, what job I should have, where I should go to college, whom I should marry, and where I should live.

When something went wrong in our lives, my mother's statement was, "It was meant to be. God is redirecting you. Something good will come of this." So, it kept us looking forward, waiting for something good to happen.

It's amazing how often God's redirection takes you to a place where something good happens because of the difficulty of the past. And, yes, I have people who call their life-threatening illness a blessing.

My father's father died when my father was twelve. There were six children and no money. To him money was to be used to make your life easier—a place to live and food on the table—so money wasn't his Lord—it wasn't about accumulating it—it was used to help people live and survive. And, he did that for his children, and he did it for lots of strangers, coworkers, and others when they were in need. He never worried about if he would be paid back—he was helping them to live. I think that rubbed off on our grandchildren, our children, and me. We live that way.

Wright

You were talking about good things coming from adversity. In a class of twenty or thirty people some time ago, my wife made a strange statement. I thought she was nuts at the time because I remembered the hell our entire family went through for such a long time during her fight with cancer. She said that even though she doesn't want cancer again, she wouldn't take a million dollars for the experience. Now she has become like a beacon of light for others going through similar circumstances.

Siegel

Ah, see, you used a lot of important words. Yes, you become a beacon—a luminary—you light the way for others, and light has no limit, it just spreads.

Referring to what your wife said, if I had to leave a message with people, I would say to pay attention to feelings and the fact that you're mortal. You see, it's hard for most people to accept the fact that, "I could really die!" You could die tomorrow; do you know what I mean? Yes, we all know that we are going to die someday, but we don't get on a plane thinking it could crash. You might think it *could* crash but there's a part of you that doesn't expect it to.

I really live with that sense of mortality—my time is precious and I don't waste my time, and I don't let other people make me miserable, and use up my time. I live my life dealing with the difficulties. If something upsets me, yes, I will work at resolving it, but I don't carry this burden of a lifetime that I hear from a lot of our group members, "My father did this, my mother did this, I got fired from my job," but it's twenty years later and they're still complaining about the same thing.

Wright

Did you always want to be a doctor when you were growing up? You were a surgeon, right?

Siegel

Yes. I am also an artist—a painter. So, I'm not a normal surgeon in terms of my personality. I became a surgeon because I had good hands; but I would say that I became a doctor for a lot of unusual reasons—reasons that most people don't normally have for becoming a doctor. I like people. On medical school applications today, there's a place to mark, "I'm fascinated by the human body." It doesn't say, "I love people." I wanted to help people. I was always oriented toward people.

The pain came when I realized that I couldn't save all the people. They were going to die no matter how good a doctor I became. And that hurt. There are no meetings at the hospital for doctors on how it feels to be a doctor and have one of your patients die. The meeting is about, "What do you think we might have done differently? Did we make any mistakes? Was it the patient's disease?" So, you're classifying things, but you never deal with feelings and, because I love people, that's where my troubles started. Then I ended up with patients and started the ECaP for support to help them. And, I'll say again, my interests were in people.

Now, I would say this to all your listeners/readers: most individuals complain about their occupation and lives because of other people. In other words, if you're a veterinarian, people bring the pets in. If you're a mortician, there are families related to the people who died. If you're a lawyer, people come in to get a divorce. So, the people are a problem. Look at your life and ask yourself, "How do I want to love the world? How do I want to help people? How do I want to serve the world in my way?" Then you can go and really enjoy your life, and don't let others impose a life on you and you lose your life.

Wright

In your organization, do you and your wife come in contact with HIV patients?

Siegel

Oh, yes. Not as much today, because there's more treatment for it, but years ago when AIDS was termed an "outbreak" we did. We supported a lot of people with AIDS because they were told, "You'll be dead quickly; there's nothing I can do for you." But, the same thing happens—if you help them with their life their immune system will improve. There are a lot of people with AIDS who aren't dead today when a doctor said they would be, and some even became HIV-negative. There wasn't an error in the lab test—they went from positive to negative with their life. Well, for one young lady with AIDS, her simple sentence was, "If you live in your heart, magic happens."

Wright

When you consider the choices you've made down through the years, has faith played an important role of your life?

Siegel

Yes, I think so. As I was mentioning earlier, I had parents who loved me, I had no trouble with the educational system, and I got along with God. I never felt that God was a punisher. Today, I use something similar to what was said many hundreds of years ago, "Disease is a loss of health." What I like to do is hold up car keys when I'm lecturing and say, "Gee, somebody dropped these in the lobby, but maybe God wants you to walk home, and so, I'm not going to return them." People laugh and I say, "Look, if you laugh at that and want your car keys, then if you lose your health, go look for it."

I think if you feel that you are a sinner, and the disease is an affliction placed upon you by God, then why get better? It's your punishment. Well, we've got enough troubles to bring us close to God; so to me, God is a resource.

Now, I think it's important for people to ask who is their Lord? I mentioned we have five children and eight grandchildren. If God came into the living room tonight and said, "I want you to sacrifice your child," what would I do? Abraham said yes. How can I say yes?

You can say yes when you know your Lord and you have faith in your Lord because, it's not out of fear that you would say yes. If Abraham had been afraid, he would have made a lot of bargains and run away and tried to hide. He might have said, "How about me and not my son?" But, he never argued nor bargained—he went in faith and knew that the good would happen.

So, I ask people, "Who is your Lord?" If it's money and the answer is, "I want a big house, I want to impress the neighbors," then you're working for the wrong Lord and you're going to do the wrong thing— you're listening to the wrong voices. But, when you have faith in the Creator and you're here to enhance life and be a co-creator and you act out of love, then I think that your faith is what's appropriate.

One of the things that drive me crazy about our planet is about religion. As a surgeon, one of my lines is, "We're all the same color inside." So, we're all from one family, but when we see religion causing us to kill each other, then that's very different. That's when I say authority and the Word becomes your Lord, and that is not about correct faith. The great prophets of the past did not create a religion so that we would kill each other—they were trying to find a path to God, and that's what we all need to find.

Wright

If you could have a platform and tell our audience something you feel would help them or encourage them, what would you say?

Siegel

Well, several things: He who seeks to save his life will lose it; he who is willing to lose his life will save it (Luke 17:33). Don't give up your life to all the authorities and then learn you're going to die and reclaim your life; live your unique life. If you do not bring forth what is within you, what you do not bring forth will destroy you. If you bring forth what is within you, what you bring forth will save you. So, pay attention to those feelings and live them and the time that you're here.

As I said, in my opinion accepting one's limited time leads one to value that time. A man who once told me he had six months to live said that time isn't money—it's everything.

Another thing I would say is to spend more time with the things and people you love or who love you and less time with those who don't love you or those you don't love.

I think those are key factors if you're going to live an authentic life. Because I love animals I'll add this: if you don't have animals in the house, adopt some because the animals and the children teach you to live in the moment.

If we have time for another story, a friend of mine learned she had a year to live. Her boyfriend couldn't deal with it emotionally, so he left her, and she was alone in her house. A cat walked across the porch and she let it in for company. She took it for a check-up the next day, and it was diagnosed with feline leukemia. She said, "I came home knowing the cat and I are going to be dead in a year. I was depressed but the cat wasn't." That cat saved her life because they're both still alive fourteen years later. I say again, live what the children and the animals know—our best day is today, let us live it fully; live in the moment, and the future will take care of itself.

Wright

Today we have been talking to Bernie Siegel, M.D. He has touched lives all across America. Thank you so much for being with us.

Siegel

My pleasure.

About The Author

BERNIE SIEGEL, M.D., is a surgeon and the author of several books on healing. His first book, *Love, Medicine and Miracles*, was considered a landmark commentary on the process of inner and outer healing. During his medical career, Dr. Siegel practiced surgery in New Haven and taught at Yale University. In 1978, he started ECaP (Exceptional Cancer Patients), a form of individual and group therapy for recovering patients.

Exceptional Cancer Patients
522 Jackson Park Drive
Meadville, PA 16335
Phone: 814.337.8192
Fax: 814.337.0699
www.ecap-online.org

Chapter 9

ARNIL NERI

THE INTERVIEW

David Wright (Wright)
Today we're talking with Arnil Neri. He is an award-winning chiropractor, a professional speaker, and author, known for his ability to ignite purpose, passion, and success in others. He is dedicated to helping others reach their maximum health potential. He earned his doctorate degree in chiropractic from New York Chiropractic College in 1994. He has been in practice for twelve years, ten of which in Woodside, Queens, New York. He has helped thousands to live better lives. Constantly striving to give his patients the most up-to-date care possible, Dr. Neri holds many post-graduate certifications in areas such as Chiropractic Pediatrics, Applied Kinesiology, and Spinal Rehabilitation.

Dr. Neri, welcome to *Dynamic Health*.

Arnil Neri (Neri)
Thank you. It is my absolute pleasure to be here.

Wright
So what is health and where does it come from? In other words, where does health and wellness begin?

Neri

In our journey in life there are things that are important to know. And there are things that are not necessary to know. For example, you don't really have to know the exact mechanism of how an airplane or a car works to use it in order to get from point A to point B. One thing important to know is how the body works because this is your main vehicle in your journey in life.

Health and wellness begins at conception and it should be maintained throughout existence. I believe that within each fertilized egg lives all the wisdom needed for the body's creation. This life force, or innate intelligence, is within every living human, animal, plant, and organism. I view it as what creates the body from a single cell to a multi-trillion-cell organism in just nine months.

This life force, or innate intelligence, did not just randomly create the body. The body evolves in a specific order. The brain, spinal cord, and nervous system were among the first organs created and these directed the formation of the other organs. As the body develops, the parts and systems form based on the body's priorities. Since the lungs of a fetus are not required until after the baby leaves the womb, the lungs are a lower priority and therefore among the last vital organs to develop fully.

The nervous system is the body's master system, controlling and coordinating all the other cells, tissues, organs, and organ systems. No cell, tissue, or organ in the body is separated from the nervous system; rather, they are an extension of your nervous system.

The nervous system is what orchestrates the healing in the body. To illustrate this truth, let me give you an experiment as an example: Take two bodies that are exactly the same except for one thing—one is alive and one is dead. Now take a knife and put a small cut on the left hand of each body. It is a common belief that external things are responsible for healing. Let's have a doctor apply an ointment like Neosporin or some type of drug to stop infection and cover it with a bandage. After two weeks, remove the bandage and what do we see? On the live body we will see a scar but on the dead body the cut will be the same as when the cut was made, however, the body will smell worse. This shows that healing only comes from within. Doctors, drugs, stitches, or bandages have no healing power without life. It is *life* that allows the body to heal. Life force flows through the nervous system distributing energy to cells and tissues in the body.

Since *life* is what controls healing, where does *life* reside in the body? When we want to check if a person is still alive or dead, what do we check for? Many of us will say the pulse or breathing, but the only way to really check for life is to see if there is any brain activity. We've seen and heard many people in what seems to be a lifeless state (not breathing and having no pulse) come back to life. As long as there is power in our brain, we are still alive. We can conclude that life is in the brain.

Healing comes from the brain and it flows from above down, inside-out. This principle is best explained by understanding cord injuries. If there is a cord injury in the lumbar spine, the body will be paralyzed from the waist down, not waist up. Similarly, if there is cord injury in the neck, as Christopher Reeves had, the body is paralyzed from the neck down—not neck up—following the above down, inside-out principle.

Another example that we can easily understand is by observing the rate of healing made by a cut in the cheek and a cut in the leg. Assuming they are of equal length and depth, which do you think would heal faster? Yes, it is the cheek because it is closer to the source of healing. You'd notice that if a man cuts himself shaving in the face, the wound heals or closes within seconds, as opposed to a cut in his leg from shaving.

Wright

Would you explain to our readers what the difference between sickness care and wellness care is?

Neri

A doctor's goal is to save and change lives. There are two ways of saving people: crisis intervention or care and preventive intervention or care. An example of crisis intervention is when someone is driving or falling off a cliff. The person could be saved by someone else reaching out and grabbing the person out of his or her predicament.

An example of preventive intervention is putting a barricade and sign to keep people from driving off the cliff—to redirect them to a different path so they can avoid the cliff.

Medicine is excellent in crisis care or sickness care while Chiropractic is excellent in wellness care. Sickness care entails symptom relief—waiting until there is a problem before taking action. Wellness care is about keeping people healthy by teaching them how to have a healthy lifestyle. Answer these questions: Does a person who has undetected cancer, although not experiencing pain, sick or healthy? Does it make sense to have pain before getting checked?

It is my belief healthy people rarely get sick and unhealthy people will be prone to sickness throughout life. People hope to avoid strokes, heart attacks, and cancer but their lifestyle choices could have them heading straight in the direction of those life-threatening conditions. People hope they won't suffer from infections, osteoarthritis, osteoporosis, high blood pressure, diabetes, and a host of other conditions. They hope their children won't be labeled with ADD, asthma, allergies, or worse.

The truth is, most hard-working, honest people today use "hope management" instead of creating wellness in their lives. Your family deserves better answers and your future depends on it.

Wright

So what are the four basic principles of chiropractic?

Neri

The first principle is based on the premise that the body is self-healing and self-regulating.

"Self-regulating" means that even when asleep, the heart continues to pump, the lungs continue to take in oxygen—there are mechanisms within the body that work without conscious effort.

"Self-healing" means our body also heals without conscious effort. When the body receives a cut, it will heal on its own. It's not the bandage or the Neosporin that makes it better—even if nothing is done to the injury, it will heal on its own. Whether the cut is on the outside (e.g., a scratch in the arm) or the inside of the body (e.g., a stomach ulcer, a cut in the stomach lining), it's the body that does the healing.

The second principle is that the nervous system is the master system of the body. The brain is where power is generated and the cord is the main information superhighway that connects the brain to the rest of the body.

The brain and the spinal cord are the only two parts of the body that are enclosed in bones because they're the most important. The brain is inside the skull and the cord is actually inside the spinal column.

The spinal column is moveable and since it's moveable, it can move out of place. When the bones move out of place it can cause nerve interference. Anything that causes interference between the communication of the brain and the body is bad. This is called Vertebral Subluxation Complex or more simply Subluxation, which is the third principle of chiropractic.

The fourth principle is anything that removes interference is good. This is what I do as a chiropractor—I remove interference in the spine by delivering a specific correction called "an adjustment."

Wright

What causes subluxations?

Neri

Specifically, physical stress, chemical stress, and mental and emotional stress are the primary causes of subluxations.

- Physical stress is basically wrong body mechanics such as improper lifting techniques, bad posture, carrying objects in the wrong way, sleeping in bad positions, being involved in motor vehicle accidents, and injuries as a result of falling.
- Chemical stress consists of poor nutrition, ingesting all kinds of drugs including alcohol, nicotine, over-the-counter and prescription drugs, pollution, and consuming processed and refined foods.
- Mental and emotional stress includes daily worries, tension, anger, fear, deadlines, finances, and grief.

All of the stressors above can cause subluxation because life is experienced through the nervous system. Any environmental changes, both external and internal are perceived and analyzed in the brain through this spinal network—therefore stress affects it.

I strongly advise patients to keep their bodies clean by reducing intake of unnecessary drugs. Sometimes, when I see patients, they are already taking maintenance drugs for their thyroid, heart, or pancreas. I don't stop them from taking those because they are necessary to keep them alive. They are already in crisis and require these drugs to balance their system chemically to live. What I do recommend against is dependence on NSAIDs (Non-Steroidal Anti-inflammatory Drugs) like acetaminophen or ibuprofen to get rid of their pain.

It is important for people to eliminate the taking of drugs because drugs are not the best way to facilitate healing. All drugs have side effects. The focus of drugs is to treat symptoms. Drugs can help one part of the body but they cause some damage in another part. Our body then will have to repair the new damaged part or organ. No wonder the sick get sicker. The body is always playing catch-up.

In the society in which we live, it is believed that the body is healed from the outside in—we are very drug oriented. As an example, upon giving birth, women receive epidurals; both the mother and child are medicated. As the child grows, he or she is immunized and given cough syrup, cold medicine, baby aspirin, and other types of drugs. By the time the child reaches early school years, sometimes he or she is put on behavioral medication. When the child reaches teenage years, he or she starts taking appetite suppressants and psychotropic drugs for depression or anxiety. Could it be that children are being conditioned during their entire life to believe pain, sickness, and behavior problems are drug deficiencies? I can assure you that headaches are not due to aspirin deficiency and muscle aches are not due to ibuprofen deficiency. In my practice, I teach people that healing is from inside out, not outside in.

Wright
How are subluxations detected and managed?

Neri
Licensed doctors of chiropractic are specially trained to detect and manage subluxations. We conduct a thorough evaluation, which includes a posture check, palpation (feeling of the spine with the hand), X-rays of the spine, and a computerized nerve test comprising of surface electromyography and thermography. A chiropractor can determine if there are any spinal misalignments and how serious they are, how many there are, and how long they have been present.

When misalignments are detected, a chiropractor will perform precise procedures called "spinal adjustments" which will be used to restore the spine to its proper position. Adjustments over time can remove the life-choking stress placed on the nervous system. By correcting and maintaining correct alignment of the spine through regular adjustments, a wellness chiropractor can help patients achieve optimal health. This could include pain relief and increased range of motion in muscles and joints. It could even improve blood circulation, reduce high blood pressure, and increase endorphin levels.

There are a number of techniques I use to adjust subluxation. These techniques differ according to the type of stress affecting the spine. There is non-force, low-force, instrument adjusting and high velocity and low impact thrusts. The techniques I use are Upper Cervical, Sacro-Occipital Technique, Chiropractic Biophysics, Activator, Diversified, Extremity adjusting, and Koren Specific Technique, which can address cranial bone misalignments as well.

Wright
What is the key to wellness care?

Neri
Most physiologists on the planet know that second by second the human body is breaking down. They also know that second by second the body is also rebuilding. The body is constantly dying but it is also constantly living. Our hair keeps on growing in that it dies and it grows. We have new skin every thirty days. We have a new liver every six weeks. We have new blood every ninety to one hundred and twenty days. Our bodies are constantly recycling.

If the body is constantly making new cells, why do people get sick? The body has memory and if communication between the brain and the body is not good it will continue to produce the same bad or poor quality cells, thereby causing deterioration. If communication is improved between the brain and the body, the body can then begin making new cells, regenerating and reversing disease processes.

When the process of breaking down is faster than the rebuilding process, the body becomes more ill. When the construction is faster than the destruction, the body stays well. Many disease processes are reversed this way. The key to wellness is a healthy nervous system.

Wright
What are the four essentials of health?

Neri
The four essentials of health and life are: food, water, air, and nerve supply. These are called essentials of health because if the body lacks these essentials, its health is reduced and it will become sick. A chronic lack of these essentials will cause death.

The average person can live without food for about forty days, it can survive up to seven days without water, three to four minutes without air, but without nerve supply—cutting off communication of the brain with the body—death is instantaneous.

I think there's a fifth essential of health, or life essential, that we all need. That is *love*. This element is most important to me because it is the glue holding everything together. Everything stems from love. After all, God is love and love brings life and love makes life worth living. Lack of self-love and love for others makes life unbearable; in fact, I firmly believe that lack of love in one's life is the biggest cause of sickness, ill health, and death.

Wright
What are the five elements of health?

Neri
I also call these elements the five keys to better health. These are also the solutions to any lack of the essentials of health. They are:

1. *A properly functioning nervous system:* The nervous system is where we experience our life. If we have a poorly functioning nervous system, we can't experience life fully. Regular spinal checkups will help keep the body functioning at an optimal level.
2. *Nutrition:* Food, water, and oxygen are basically the most important elements that the body must have.
   - Every cell in the body uses oxygen; it is disbursed by the pulmonary, lungs, and circulatory systems. Interference with these systems can impede oxygen travel and significantly affect the body. One way to stimulate more complete oxygen intake is through breathing exercises.
   - Water is essential for good health. Seventy-five percent of the body is water. One-half the body's weight is the number of ounces the body requires of water every day. For example, if a person is one hundred and eighty pounds, the amount of water needed by that individual is ninety ounces. Another way to be sure the body is getting enough water is to check the color of the urine. If it is clear, the body is getting enough water. If the urine is yellow to dark amber, that may indicate some dehydration.
   - Food is the fuel needed for growth and reproduction of cells and tissues. Poor nutrition leads to poor health. An imbalance can occur from consuming too much fat or too little essential fat or too much sugar or too much salt. For good nutrition, eat as many raw fruits

and vegetables as possible. Eliminate processed foods, which will cut down on the consumption of chemicals you will unknowingly be putting in your body.

3. *Exercise:* Motion creates emotion. A California State University study found that a ten-minute walk is enough to increase energy, alter mood, and effect a positive outlook for up to two hours. I recommend that all my patients exercise a minimum of three times a week for at least thirty minutes.

4. *Rest:* The body repairs itself during rest, so it is important to have good rest. A good sleeping position is the key to good rest. When sleeping on your stomach you will experience poor rest because you are compressing your organs. Better positions are on your back or on your side.

5. *Positive mental attitude:* Laugh and smile often. Have faith—connect with your Creator. Remember, the power that made your body heals your body. Be grateful and love every minute of life.

Remember, no one else can be responsible for your health and the health of your family. Choose to take control and be proactive; practice the five keys to better health.

Wright
Will you explain to our readers who can benefit from chiropractic care?

Neri
Anybody can benefit from chiropractic care because everyone has a spine that can become stressed. Remember, stress causes subluxation. People of all ages come to see me with an array of health challenges, everything from headaches and migraines, seizures and seizure disorders, fibromyalgia, fatigue, acid reflux, esophageal spasms, lupus, sleeping disorders, allergies, bilateral carpal tunnel syndrome, and even ADD or hyperactivity. Patients with these conditions and symptoms have one thing in common—subluxations. Once their subluxations were corrected they experienced a better quality of life.

Wright
Let me get this straight; are you telling me that if my spine is not healthy, it prevents my body from running properly, and without sub-

luxations I have a better chance of great body function, good health, and a longer healthier life?

Neri

Absolutely! Chiropractic is a method of keeping the body working well by eliminating interference to the nervous system's control of normal function.

Many people think that chiropractic is just for taking care of neck pain and back pain because chiropractic has been shown to be excellent for pain relief. But there are more benefits in chiropractic than just relief.

The true value of chiropractic is in improving overall performance. It improves ones reflexes, it removes brain fog, and allows the organ systems to function efficiently.

Let chiropractic help you to be a more productive worker, a quicker and stronger athlete, a loving spouse, a nurturing parent, and an attentive student. Let chiropractic help you be the best that you can be.

Wright

Why do chiropractors recommend lifetime wellness care?

Neri

True health comes from within and by doing the right things long enough. No one would brush and floss for a number of years only to stop one day and never brush again for the next thirty years. The damage to the teeth would be severe. It is exactly the same way with corrective chiropractic—only by identifying, addressing, and correcting physical, mental, and chemical stressors will you be able to achieve maximum health potential in mind, body, and spirit.

Healing is a process and any process takes time. We have become accustomed to expect quick fixes. We take pills for any kind of condition. I question again the outside-in health philosophy. I don't believe there is a pill, potion, or lotion with better odds of improving health than your deciding to help yourself from the inside out.

True health takes time to achieve and can be lost so quickly. Imagine committing to exercise for ten years and then stopping suddenly. The benefits of ten years of fitness will be lost in a matter of weeks. The same is true for most activities that contribute to health such as brushing the teeth, spiritual practices, regular exercise, lifetime weekly chiropractic adjustments, and eating clean food from health food stores. Illness takes time to heal; a loss of health does not happen overnight, even though it may seem to have snuck up on you. A loss of health could be a result of subluxations and bad habits accumulating over time.

Regardless of what everyone else is doing, accept the fact that healing does not come from the outside and it doesn't happen overnight. The only place you'll find healing is within your body, your mind, and your spirit. Take care of them by practicing healthy habits for the rest of your life. Embrace this and you'll find your new life could be far better.

Wright

So what is the mission of your chiropractic office?

Neri

Our mission is to educate and do spinal adjustments on as many families as possible to help them toward optimal health through our very specific natural corrective chiropractic approach. Education is as important as the care itself because when people understand how the body works, then they become proactive in achieving their maximum health potential without becoming too dependent on medical doctors.

Subluxations controlled through regular chiropractic checkups can result in less chance of damage. Wellness is a proactive process, not a reactive event. We can help our body optimize its natural healing abilities by removing subluxations. My purpose as a chiropractor is to help enable people to express 100 percent true health and wellness, reaching their fullest life potential. This is my commitment to my patients and to my family.

The greatest gift you can give your loved ones is a complete spinal evaluation by a doctor of chiropractic. Chiropractic is about living a higher quality of life and should be the first choice on the path toward wellness.

To end, I'd like to quote D. D. Palmer, the founder of chiropractic. He said, "To adjust the subluxation then, is to advance mankind, step up his efficiency, increase his ability, make him more natural and at peace with himself."

Now that you have learned the meaning of chiropractic, don't keep it to yourself. You can educate and inform others.

Wright

One final question: will you share with us the secret of your success with patients?

Neri

Tell the truth, educating and providing an environment of love is the secret. Love is a balance of support and challenge. Too little challenge and too much support make one weak and dependent. On the other hand, too much challenge and very little support makes one rebellious. I challenge my patients by telling them things they might not necessarily want to hear but that I know are essential for their growth and healing. At the same time I support whatever decisions they make.

Another ingredient of success is just having fun. I love being a health coach to my patients. I tell them to have fun and not get caught in just making a living—they should be involved in designing their life and practice the chiropractic lifestyle.

Lastly, our practice adapts to change. Our office is constantly evolving. Our practice is different today compared to ten years ago or even five years ago. We regularly attend post-graduate seminars and study and refine our chiropractic adjusting techniques. We do all these things so we can provide the best and highest quality care to our patients.

Wright

Today we have been talking with Dr. Arnil Neri. The interesting thing I have found about Dr. Neri is that he takes genuine interest in his patients' care. His office focuses on the total health of the individual, not just the integrity of the spine. In addition to chiropractic care he offers his patients nutritional counseling, physical therapy, wellness, and other alternative health care techniques that enable them to improve their health and the health of their families naturally.

Dr. Neri, thank you so much for taking all this time to answer these questions and for being with us today on *Dynamic Health*.

About the Author

DR. ARNIL NERI is a student of universal truths and principles. When he discovered the chiropractic truth, the science, art, and philosophy of healing without drugs or surgery, he embraced it completely. His mission is to make chiropractic known and available to everyone especially in his birthplace, the Philippines.

Dr. Arnil Neri
50-11 Queens Boulevard,
Woodside, NY 11377
Telephone: 718.507.2427
Fax: 718.507.4539
E-mail: DrArnil@earthlink.net
www.NeriChiro.net

Chapter 10

IAN WAHL, PH.D., LAC, CH

THE INTERVIEW

David Wright (Wright)
Today we're talking with Ian Wahl, Ph.D, LAc, CH. Ian and the Natural Fertility Health Centers of America are pioneering the Integrated Dynamic Fertility program. Fertility problems arise from imbalances in the network of organs, hormones, and energy systems within a woman's or a man's body. The core of the program is an individualized treatment plan, which includes acupuncture, diet therapy, lifestyle considerations, self-massage and breathing techniques, structural balancing, herbs, healing affirmations and visualizations, therapeutic grade essential oils, and spiritual awareness exercises. Integrated Dynamic Fertility combines the use of natural health care, prayer, and spiritual awareness to successfully enhance the fertility of couples naturally or in conjunction with Western fertility treatments.

Ian Wahl, welcome to *Dynamic Health.*

Ian Wahl (Wahl)
Thank you very much, David.

Wright

Before we get into your specialty of reproductive Oriental medicine and acupuncture to treat fertility problems, will you explain what you mean by "Oriental medicine" and acupuncture?

Wahl

Scholars say that Oriental medicine is almost 5,000 years old. In fact, the Huang Di Nei Jing or the *Yellow Emperor's Internal Medicine Classic* on which traditional Chinese medicine is based, is dated around 2600 B.C.E. Often you'll hear the term "Oriental medicine" used synonymously with the term "traditional Chinese medicine" or with the initials TCM. I also use them interchangeably, so that's what I'm going to do as we're talking today. Experts say it is the oldest, literate, continually practiced medicine in the world. Currently over one quarter of the world's population uses it. You can say with confidence that modern Western and traditional Oriental medicines are the two dominant medical paradigms in the world today.

There are seven branches to Oriental medicine. These are acupuncture, herbal medicine, nutrition and dietary counseling, exercise and movement therapy, massage, relaxation techniques (including meditation and spiritual awareness practices), and feng shui (environmental considerations—how the physical environment is set up around a person). These seven branches of Oriental medicine (TCM) comprise a system that is based upon the principle that in order to be healthy, a human must be balanced physically, mentally, emotionally, and spiritually. Imbalances are caused by blockages in the flow of a measurable energy (*Qi*) that travels through the body. This energy, or Qi, moves the blood, which is vital to normal organ and tissue function. Good health is dependent upon the flow of Qi through the body. A blockage of Qi can cause pain, disease, or a multitude of other conditions. In other words, TCM theory states that the body's tissues and organs need to have a proper balance of blood, oxygen, nutrients, and hormones flowing unobstructed and in a homeostatic balance.

This sounds like a bit like Western medicine, however this balance, according to TCM theory, is kept functioning by the smooth flow of Qi or energy. Acupuncture in particular deals with over 2,000 specific points that have been mapped out on the body. Interestingly enough, these points are located where nerves and blood vessels happen to meet. So, when there is a blockage in the flow of Qi and/or blood in the body, dis-ease can occur and a trained acupuncturist can diagnose which points to treat to increase the flow of Qi or blood which allows successful results with all types of health problems, whether acute or chronic.

This may sound confusing, so I'm going to give a simple analogy. Let's look at a plant that was deprived of water. Without water a plant would wither and die. If you tried to water that plant with a hose that had a kink or blockage preventing water from getting through, then the plant would still die. Remove the blockage and give the plant water and it will recover. Acupuncture and Oriental medicine finds where the blockage is in the body that stops life-giving blood, oxygen, nutrients, and hormones from flowing through your organs, tissues, and cells, and it unblocks it.

Thousands of years ago the Yellow Emperor, in his internal medicine classic, used a different analogy. We know that great civilizations arose around rivers because the fresh water flowing through the river nourished the land, the plants, the people, etc. The Yellow Emperor took that concept and imagined rivers running through the body. He called them "meridians"—pathways. Along these meridians are located the 2,000 acupuncture points. Each of these points, along a given meridian, has a different function that affects specific organs within the body. Though you can't see meridians, you can experience their functioning. It's similar to when the ground shifts during an earthquake. One can feel the ground move many miles away from the actual area of the earthquake itself. Acupuncture meridians work in a similar fashion. Even though we can't see the meridians, we can experience their effect.

Actually, everybody's experienced this concept—even you, David. How many times have you found that a shoulder massage or a foot massage can help you with a headache? That's why we can put a needle in someone's foot or leg to treat his/her neck, shoulder, or head and the person experiences relief.

I specialize in treating couples experiencing fertility issues. Many of my patients come to me after they have exhausted tens of thousands of dollars and have yet to either conceive a child or have miscarried. Though patients can't see what's happening in their bodies when an acupuncture needle is inserted, they certainly can see the results when their baby is born. Millions of babies have been born over thousands of years with the use of acupuncture, Oriental medicine, and herbs.

Wright

Is there a modern scientific explanation of acupuncture?

Wahl

Actually, there is. The most current scientific hypothesis is that needling acupuncture points stimulates the nervous system to release chemicals in the muscles, the spinal cord, and the brain. These chemicals either change the experience of pain or trigger the release of other chemicals—neurotransmitters and hormones—influencing the body's own internal regulating system. The improved energy and hormonal balance produced by acupuncture stimulates the body's own natural healing abilities and promotes physical and emotional well-being and health. In other words, acupuncture stimulates the immune system of the body to heal itself from the inside out.

Wright

What does all this have to do with infertility?

Wahl

That's a good question. Fertility is the natural condition of a healthy woman of childbearing age. Now, I'm going to make a really bold statement that surprises people when I say it. There are very, *very* few infertile women; most are just out of balance.

Our Integrated Dynamic Fertility program, which is based upon Oriental medicine, removes the blockages that cause imbalances in the flow of blood, oxygen, nutrients, and hormones. During our treatments, and even before a woman becomes pregnant, she'll usually experience relief of other symptoms she may have had such as headaches, digestive problems, fatigue, sleep problems, PMS, menstrual irregularities, mood swings, etc.

Infertility in America affects fifteen to 20 percent of us. Some women have mechanical dysfunctions such as severe and long-term tubal obstructions, previous hysterectomies, and other physiological conditions that make natural and unassisted conception impossible.

That said, I have not met many women, who have all of their reproductive organs anatomically functioning, who cannot get pregnant. There are many reasons a couple has difficulty conceiving but most of them can be overcome and conception can occur. When physical, mental, emotional, and spiritual balance is restored women of childbearing age can return to their natural fertile state.

There are souls—spirits of babies—waiting to be born and they're looking for a healthy nurturing mother to open her arms and her womb and accept them. By bringing the entire body back into balance—by restoring hormonal harmony—women can find their natural fertility is restored.

Wright
You mentioned herbs earlier. How do these play a role in treating fertility?

Wahl
Acupuncture and herbal medicine work together to restore optimal functioning to a person but they work very differently. Acupuncture needles increase the flow of blood, oxygen, nutrients, and energy through the body. Herbal medicines, however, are just that—plants, roots, stems, leaves, minerals, etc., that are taken internally as medicine. Whereas acupuncture enhances circulation and blood flow, herbs are natural energetic substances that gently correct underlying deficiencies and clear obstructions.

At our clinic we base herbal formulas on the individual's diagnostic pattern. We use different herbal formulas at different times during a woman's cycle. I need to make one thing clear: the success we have in our clinic is grounded in the principle that acupuncture and herbal medicine are only part of the program. Although we individualize our treatment plans, the ultimate goal is to restore hormonal harmony, rebalance the body's energies, and prepare a woman's body to nurture a child from conception through the birth of a healthy baby.

The foundation of our program, which I call Integrated Dynamic Fertility, involves the evaluation and treatment of the human body's four-part ecosystem—the hormone/immune system, the biomechanical system, the energetic/meridian system, and the mental/spiritual system. By aligning health in all four systems, a woman's body becomes balanced, working properly as a whole, providing good health and fertility as a natural byproduct.

This is achieved by incorporating a number of modalities including Oriental medicine, acupuncture, herbal and diet therapy. We teach self-massage, relaxation and stress reduction techniques, exercise and stretching techniques, meditative, spiritual, and healing visualizations, structural balancing and soft tissue therapy, and therapeutic grade essential oils. Everything is based on the time-tested methods of Oriental medicine.

The process we go through is simple: We first diagnose what's going on so we can determine what needs to be harmonized. We explore dietary recommendations based on our diagnosis, and this usually includes recommending supplements also. We unblock the energy pathways of the body with a combination of acupuncture, exercises, massage, and structural balancing to get the Qi flowing smoothly again and thus balance out the energy meridians. We use safe and effective herbal formulas that have been used for thousands and thousands of years to help increase fertility.

We continually assess our progress, revise our formulas and treatment protocols as needed, and we help balance a woman's body so she is in harmony with the universe and ready to receive the soul of a child in her womb.

Wright

I'm sure that many of your patients are seeing Western fertility doctors. Do you ever work in concert with them or coordinate your treatments with them?

Wahl

Absolutely, we do. There's an old Chinese proverb that goes something like this, "There are many paths to the top of a mountain, but the view is always the same."

I prefer to see couples conceive without the use of dangerous drugs and excessive amounts of hormones injected into their bodies. However, I know that sometimes there are mechanical and anatomically organic reasons why a woman will not be able to conceive. I personally have seen women in our practice who have had severe tubal obstructions—and even women who don't have any tubes at all but who still have an ovary and a uterus—who will never be able to conceive naturally, but they can still give birth to their own child. These women need to see a reproductive endocrinologist—a Western fertility doctor. Our treatments will support the woman, physically, mentally, emotionally, and spiritually through the fertility procedures. In fact, our Integrated Dynamic Fertility program prepares the woman's body and spirit for Western fertility treatments, relieves the side effects of the medications given, and increases the chances of successful conception and birth by 60 to 90 percent.

Most of the women in our clinic have sought us out after repeated failure of ART (Assisted Reproductive Technology), better known as Western fertility treatments such as artificial insemination, and in vitro fertilization (IVF), among other types of treatments.

The follicular genesis cycle is about ninety days. Therefore, I tell my patients that it is better to begin our treatments at least ninety days, or three menstrual cycles, before they start their ART treatments. This enables us to balance and harmonize the body's energy, blood, and organ functions to produce the best possible ART response. A woman wants to be as hormonally balanced and as physically, mentally, emotionally, and spiritually healthy as possible before any invasive medical intervention, especially one involving the injection of massive amounts of hormones.

The funny thing is, many of our patients get pregnant during the three months before they have their ART procedures. Once a woman's underlying root cause for her fertility problems are uncovered and dealt with, conception can occur naturally most of the time.

I want to further address the question you asked about the process of working with a Western fertility doctor. At the Natural Fertility Health Centers, we first send a letter to the patient's doctor informing them we're working with their patient. We encourage our patients to consult their reproductive endocrinologist (RE) before beginning treatment with us, but just to make sure we send out that letter. Most doctors are open to our treatments with their patients. We receive many referrals from reproductive endocrinologists within the Chicago area. Most REs appreciate our focus on stress reduction and relieving the side effects of their medications and procedures.

We emphasize stress reduction because ART is very stressful for the woman. Where we differ from reproductive endocrinologists, however, is that we work a woman long after she has conceived. We continue to treat her through her pregnancy and even postpartum. At that point we work with the obstetrician (OB) and/or midwife, staying in touch with them through the pregnancy. Our patients' doctors have remarked many times how often our patients have had model pregnancies right out of a textbook. This is due to keeping the woman's body in balance throughout the pregnancy. The birth and postpartum period is also medically uneventful and thus it's pleasurable for the new mom and the new dad.

Wright

What about men? I've heard that many men have fertility problems too.

Wahl

It's funny and sad and one thing people don't like to talk about. Statistics in the U.S. show that up to 40 percent of couples experiencing fertility problems have factors that involve both the man and the woman.

There are three major factors in male infertility: not enough sperm (low sperm count); motility insufficiency (the sperm does not move forward as it should); or the sperm is shaped abnormally (poor sperm morphology). If the sperm is not shaped correctly it cannot penetrate the egg. Almost two hundred million sperm are ejaculated at a time but only a few dozen actually reach the egg and then they have to work their way into fertilizing the egg.

Believe it or not, sperm counts have dropped 50 percent in the last thirty to forty years, depending on the study you read. Sperm counts can be further lowered by factors such as stress, poor diet, prescription drugs—blood pressure meds, pain meds—over-the-counter antihistamines, alcohol, nicotine, and marijuana.

Although these male factors are easier to diagnose through Western medicine, Western medicine has a difficult time treating them successfully. The good news is that our natural treatments have great success reversing low sperm count and poor sperm quality. All it takes is small but significant changes to a man's diet and lifestyle and, when combined with acupuncture and herbs, it can make a remarkable difference. Not only do those treatments help balance the hormonal system but they also help raise virility levels in men.

Unfortunately, there's a particular type of male factor that is not treatable with Oriental medicine or with the Integrated Dynamic Fertility program. A congenital problem known as azoospermia— complete absence of sperm—has no known cure. That condition is not the same as low sperm count due to stress, whether it's physical, chemical, or emotional. Any stress related sperm conditions respond extremely well to acupuncture, herbs, diet, and lifestyle changes.

Wright

Do you mean the body just simply doesn't manufacture any sperm?

Wahl

That's right. It's not common but it's a condition that is real. When male sterility is detected, a doctor is going to explore further to see why. Oftentimes it is due to something such as a varicocele, which is like a varicose vein on a testicle, or a hydrocele, which is just a fluid filled cyst in the testicles. These types of varicose veins and cysts are not dangerous—they just raise the scrotal temperature, which kills off the sperm. Many times, varicoceles and hydroceles respond well to acupuncture, Oriental medicine, diet, and lifestyle changes.

Wright

Are you saying that there are times when acupuncture, herbs, and your Integrated Dynamic Fertility program won't help a patient conceive a baby?

Wahl

You need to have the plumbing in place for your bathroom faucet to work. I already mentioned the case where the male factor problems aren't amenable. And when there's something wrong with the woman's reproductive organs—some anatomical anomaly or missing organs—we just can't help them conceive naturally. Often however, these problems can be surgically handled with TCM and Integrated Dynamic Fertility used as an adjunct treatment. For example, a severely tilted uterus—one that is tipped back so far that the sperm can't reach the egg—can be surgically corrected. But a woman who has never had a complete biomedical fertility workup can't know whether she has something mechanically/anatomically wrong.

While there may be some physiological conditions that prevent women from conceiving naturally, they can still benefit from TCM and Integrated Dynamic Fertility. The benefits to harmonizing and balancing the hormone system, structurally integrating the body, learning how to relieve stress, and dealing with the emotional and spiritual aspects of fertility problems are enormous. We have even seen severe endometriosis resolve and the woman become pregnant and give birth to a beautiful little boy.

As with all medical procedures, however, there are no guarantees. Any medicine, no matter what it is, doesn't work every time. Whether you're given a muscle relaxer for a backache or receive open-heart surgery, no biomedical Western physician can guarantee their medication or that their procedures will be 100 percent effective. The same thing applies to Oriental medicine—it isn't always 100 percent clinically effective; but there are no side effects and there are many, many subclinical benefits felt when a human being experiences restored balance and health. A good acupuncturist, like a good medical doctor, has to know what they can and what they cannot treat. Our training is such that we know when to refer to a specialist or to a Western medical doctor.

Wright

What kind of education and training is required in Oriental medicine and acupuncture? How does the prospective patient pick someone qualified?

Wahl

Regarding your first question, I'll put it this way: most people are unaware that an acupuncturist is required to complete a four-year postgraduate degree in Oriental medicine. An acupuncturist's medical education is devoted to scientific subjects such as anatomy, biochemistry, microbiology, pathology, even pharmacology, public health diagnosis, other clinical disciplines, and other health sciences in addition to the study of acupuncture and herbal medicine. A key component of the training is a multi-year clinical internship to fully ensure a graduate has the technical expertise and experience to successfully treat patients.

Your question about how to choose someone qualified is quite relevant. First, you have to make certain the acupuncturist has been fully trained in Oriental medicine and has graduated from a nationally accredited graduate school of Oriental medicine and acupuncture. Be sure the practitioner is a state licensed acupuncturist, a nationally board certified acupuncturist, holds a Diplomate of Acupuncture, and has specialized training in herbal medicine.

Many practitioners of acupuncture have taken weekend courses and have received certifications that are not recognized by the National Certification Commission for Acupuncture and Oriental Medicine (NCCAOM). Acupuncture and Oriental medicine is an extremely complicated and extensive medical system. It is not just a collection of techniques that can be added to some other healthcare profession. Just as you would not seek an internist to perform brain surgery, one should only seek treatment from professionally trained and qualified practitioners of acupuncture and Oriental medicine.

There's one more point I'd like to make regarding this. Most acupuncturists (in fact, almost all of them) are generalists—they treat everything. Remember, acupuncture and Oriental medicine is a complete medicine. Just as Western medicine treats so much more than cancer and major surgery or emergency room issues, the National Institutes of Health and the World Health Organization have identified scores of diseases and conditions that lend themselves to acupuncture and Oriental medicine treatments. These conditions include everything from infections to internal medicine, from musculoskelotal conditions to neurological problems, eye, ear, nose and throat conditions to dermatology, to mental/emotional problems, as well as gynecology and reproductive medicine.

When it comes to fertility treatments, however, there's a certain amount of expertise and experience required. This is especially relevant because many of the women we deal with have become very fragile after spending so much time feeling they have failed as a woman. You need to make sure your practitioner has the right experience. Just as you'd rather see a reproductive endocrinologist rather than your family practice doctor for fertility treatments, you need to see an acupuncturist who has a track record of specialized practice for natural fertility treatments also.

Most good acupuncturists and herbalists may be technically competent but if they don't integrate the spiritual component into their practice, they should not be your first choice for fertility treatments.

Wright

Now that you've mentioned the spirituality component, how do address spirituality?

Wahl

The Harvard Medical School just completed a study recently published in a journal of the American Society of Reproductive Medicine. The study evaluated 200 infertile women. It indicated that a high level of spiritual well-being is linked to increased fertility. That study also found, however, that many physicians do not describe themselves as personally spiritual and thus do not feel comfortable talking with women about spiritual issues.

Spirituality, healing visualization, and increasing the awareness and acknowledgment of a women's fertile soul build the framework of our Integrated Dynamic Fertility program.

This is especially important for patients who are undergoing Western fertility treatments because the spirits and souls of babies are hesitant to enter an embryo that is being developed artificially in a petri dish. They want the warmth and nurturing of a loving receptive womb. Whether a woman is trying to conceive naturally or with ART, we teach her (and her partner) to get in touch with the spirit and soul of their baby to assure their child awaiting birth that he or she is loved, wanted, and will be lovingly placed within Mommy's nurturing womb as soon as possible. That may sound New Age or like it's far out there; but when couples come to us for fertility treatments, I explain the concepts of the fertile soul and spirit babies the very first time I meet with them. And I've never had one person look at me and say, "You're nuts. I'm outta here!" Instead, they begin to understand the difference between our approach and the rest of the acupuncturists they have interviewed.

We call ourselves a FertileSpirit™ clinic. This is a critical part of our program. These retreats are offered at a resort spa and they integrate the concepts of mind, body, spirit, and healing with an understanding that there is hope for the couple experiencing fertility problems. That hope requires a paradigm shift in their way of thinking. After explaining the TCM approach to fertility treatments we help open their hearts and minds to prayerful healing visualization and affirmations to open themselves to accept the soul of a baby waiting to be born. Our philosophy is that we were here before, we're coming back again, and we don't come back as adults; we come back as babies—our souls do anyway. We use the spa experience to make the weekend as mentally relaxing and emotionally nourishing as possible. We then follow up with regular visits at our clinic after the FertileSpirit™ retreat to sustain the continuity of care.

It doesn't matter what your religious belief is, there is a universal source of healing that envelops us all. That universal source of healing is not judgmental and does not care whether a man or woman has led an exemplary life. When a person's body is balanced physically, mentally, emotionally, and spiritually, that person becomes aware of the universal source of healing. Whether a person calls it prayer, healing affirmations, or guided visualizations, we provide the safe environment and caring help to teach a woman to forgive herself and to nourish and develop her fertile soul. We work with the parents-to-be on their nurturing self-image.

Wright

When someone comes to your clinic for help, how do you put it all together? What can they expect?

Wahl

First, we have the couple complete lengthy, detailed fertility and health history questionnaires. These questionnaires will help us determine their energetic pattern of disturbance so we can develop a treatment plan based on their underlying root causes of disharmony.

After the paperwork is completed, the couple is taken into a consultation room. And, by the way, we encourage fertility patients to come with their husbands for the first consultation/evaluation. We consider it critical that the couple be together because we've noticed our most successful patients are the ones who come with their husbands during the first consultation.

During that initial consultation/evaluation we go through the health history and fertility questionnaires in detail. I may ask the patient and her husband a multitude of questions in addition to those on the questionnaires. However, before I even look at the health and fertility questionnaires, I ask the patient to tell me her fertility story—what was her journey that led her to my office. David, these stories can often break your heart. I usually ask the woman whether her dominant desire is to be a mother or to give birth. Those are different paths for different couples.

After this consultation I briefly explain the history of Oriental medicine and fertility treatments. Then I perform a complete Oriental medical exam including pulse and tongue diagnosis. I'll quickly explain what I mean by "pulse and tongue diagnosis." There are twelve major meridian pathways in the body that the Chinese identified. We can assess the function of those major meridians and the organs they are associated with through pulses. There are twenty-eight different pulse qualities. One is normal and nobody has a normal pulse all the time. The other twenty-seven indicate some disharmony or dysfunction in the body. We also look at the tongue—the shape, coating, size, color, and geography. Are there cracks? Where are the cracks? Are there specific markings on the tongue? Is it predominately wet or dry, etc.? These tongue conditions all mean something that could be used to complete a diagnosis based upon the pattern exhibited by the patient through the pulse and the tongue, their symptoms, and other issues. These patterns have been empirically observed and recorded by TCM doctors for thousands of years.

By the time we've completed our consultation and exam, I know enough about the patient to determine if I feel comfortable treating them and they know enough about me, our clinic, and the Integrated Dynamic Fertility program to make an informed decision whether to continue or not. If they choose to continue I put together an individualized treatment plan, including acupuncture, nutritional recommendations, self-massage techniques, structural balancing and soft tissue therapy, herbs, healing affirmations and visualizations, essential oil therapy, as well as the spiritual awareness exercises and practices. The treatment plan is flexible and customized to the patient's diagnostic pattern as well as to her decision whether to combine Western fertility treatments with our natural methods.

This initial visit usually lasts one and one-half to two hours. Subsequent visits are approximately forty-five to sixty minutes long, depending upon the amount of emotional support the patient required that day. We include emotional support in our treatments.

By the way, many people are afraid of needles. I tell patients that acupuncture needles are about the twice the thickness of a human hair and they aren't like hypodermic needles—they aren't hollow. We use only the highest quality, sterile, disposable, stainless steel needles. While the patient is lying on the table during acupuncture, he/she is in a dimly lit room with soothing, relaxing music playing in the background. The experience is so pleasant that many patients actually fall asleep during treatment which is really when self-healing can begin.

Once the couple decides to become patients, the treatment plan is presented, and we begin to work on lifestyle modifications directly related to both stress reduction and fertility. We use massage and structural balancing therapy to help relieve the physical, mental, and chemical stresses of the Western fertility treatments, if that's what they've chosen. Acupuncture will improve the blood flow to the uterus and ovaries and helps prepare the uterus for implantation and pregnancy. It also calms the mother-to-be and allows her to better deal with the stresses of Western fertility treatments, if she has chosen to go that route, or just with the stresses of fertility issues in general. The herbal treatments deal with the woman's underlying balance and they will naturally balance her hormonal cycle.

The threads of the tapestry of our Integrated Dynamic Fertility program are all sown together with our fertility retreats and our healing spiritual awareness practices and visualizations in concert with the use of therapeutic grade essential oils that work on an emotional level with the mother-to-be to bring her back in touch with her fertile soul.

Wright

It certainly sounds like you spend much more time with the patient than the typical medical doctor. What exactly makes your fertility treatment unique?

Wahl

That's an interesting observation and a good question. The Western medical paradigm is very different from the Oriental medical paradigm. Western medicine is the best at identifying and minutely measuring the smallest details of disease. The diagnostic and clinical tests and measurements of blood, hormone levels, DNA, the results of CAT scans, PET scans, and ultrasounds, can tell us a great deal about what's going on at the microscopic level. That's why we have the best diagnostic medicine in the world here in America. I'd never want to see us give up Western medicine. Sometimes, however, Western medicine can't see the forest for the trees they're analyzing.

On the other hand, Oriental medicine and Integrated Dynamic Fertility in particular, is much more holistic. It allows us to establish a relationship with patients in which we can have an ongoing dialog throughout the course of treatment. For many patients, "The Wahls of Wellness," our affiliated family healthcare clinic, become their primary care physicians after the birth of their baby. If they have a condition we cannot be successful in treating, we refer them to Western medical care. And that's the way it should be—you should try a natural solution first before embarking on medications that can have side effects.

I'd like to amplify something I just mentioned. I said that our Integrated Dynamic Fertility treatments are more holistic. By "holistic" I mean treating the whole person. In Western medicine the emphasis is on treating the disease, or the symptoms of the disease, whereas we treat the whole person as the dynamic that needs to be brought back into harmony and balance. Many practitioners claim to be holistic but they do not address the entire balance of the human ecosystem—only parts of it. Our uniqueness is our Integrated Dynamic Fertility program.

I'm going to give you an example. Someone may have a fertility problem caused by the enormous stress of his or her job. All the artificial hormones in the world aren't going to address that. Neither is combining some needles with herbal formulas, throwing in a bit of Yoga, or giving them a massage. The patient has to be brought to the awareness that something in their lifestyle is interfering with the four pillars of their human ecosystem—their hormone/immune system, biomechanical system, energetic/meridian system, and mental/spiritual system. These all act upon and influence one another.

A 2001 study from the University of California, San Diego, concluded that women with the highest rated life stress levels were 93 percent less likely to become pregnant and carry to term than those women who scored lower on the stress scale. Our unique holistic approach directly addresses stress reduction and puts it into perspective with the patient's physiological, chemical, emotional, and spiritual conditions. In other words, we actually teach people to balance their human eco-system.

And that is why couples have been successfully having children after coming to our clinic when they were not successful in other clinics. We see couples after they have been through the emotional wringer of infertility. We see women desperate to conceive yet physically and emotionally traumatized by their experiences through Western fertility treatments. We see couples just before they are ready to give up trying to have their own baby. We counsel those who feel like complete failures as women. We watch them struggle as they attempt to balance their lives and time to include our fertility retreats, our recommended diets, lifestyle changes, acupuncture treatments, massage and structural balancing and soft tissue therapies, affirmations, herbs and supplements. And then we watch with awe as they forgive themselves and no longer place blame for their fertility problems. We witness their transformation into a spiritual awareness that allows them to touch the very souls of babies waiting to be born. We journey with them as they come to terms with their own fertile souls. And we hold them as they cry tears of joy when they tell us they are pregnant. And, still, after all these years, we also cry tears of joy with them. But the best part is when we get to hold their miracle babies in our arms. We have the best job in the world and wouldn't give it up for anything. And maybe that's what really makes us unique.

Wright

Today we have been talking with Ian Wahl. He recommends the Integrated Dynamic Fertility program that combines the use of natural healthcare, prayer, and spiritual awareness to successfully enhance the fertility of couples naturally or in conjunction with Western fertility treatments.

Ian, this has been an enlightening conversation. I really appreciate all this time you've spent with me to answer these questions. I'm sure our readers are going to be fascinated and instructed by your chapter.

Thank you so much for being with us on *Dynamic Health*.

About The Author

DR. IAN WAHL, founder and director of the Natural Fertility Health Centers, specializes in reproductive wellness and women's health. His successful Integrated Dynamic Fertility™ program offers a unique blending of Eastern and Western medicine integrated with essential oils, healing meditations, and spiritual awareness practices. Dr. Wahl is a licensed acupuncturist, trained in herbal medicine and nutrition, an author and lecturer, a professional member of RESOLVE, The National Infertility Association, and the American Society for Reproductive Medicine.

Ian Wahl, Ph.D., LAc, CH
Natural Fertility Health Centers
3375 N. Arlington Heights Road, Suite A
Arlington Heights, IL 60004
Phone: 847 392-7901
Fax: 847 392-7921
Email: ian@NaturalFertilityHealthCenters.com
www.NaturalFertilityHealthCenters.com